ZERO HOUR

ZERO HOUR

A Summons to the Free

by

STEPHEN VINCENT BENÉT
ERIKA MANN
McGEORGE BUNDY
WILLIAM L. WHITE
GARRETT UNDERHILL
WALTER MILLIS

Essay Index Reprint Series

BOOKS FOR LIBRARIES PRESS
FREEPORT, NEW YORK

First Published 1940
Reprinted 1971

INTERNATIONAL STANDARD BOOK NUMBER:
0-8369-2341-3

LIBRARY OF CONGRESS CATALOG CARD NUMBER:
71-156734

PRINTED IN THE UNITED STATES OF AMERICA

CONTENTS

I

SIX OF US TALKING

Stephen Vincent Benét

I

SIX OF US TALKING

I

THERE is a crisis in our national life and it is now. It is not tomorrow or the day after tomorrow but now. How long it will last, not one of us can say. But, while it lasts, it will touch the thoughts, the acts and the day-to-day lives of all of us.

We have not been a complacent country—not these last ten years. We have criticized ourselves for doing things even while we were doing them and, at times, produced the impression of a pair of Siamese twins, trying to go in several directions at once. All the same, we have been largely concentrated on our own internal problems and how to meet them. In spite of individual Cassandras, in spite of warnings from men in responsible positions, we have kept our eyes turned on our own back yard, not across the water. In spite of political yells from political extremists, we have—a great many millions of us—taken democracy for granted, not merely as a way of life but as the good way of life—the one way of life for free and rational men.

Now that proposition has been challenged, not only passively but actively, not only by propaganda but by force. With a sense of incredulous shock, we have seen war shake the world again and a new world-revolution on the march.

That was the first and understandable reaction—shock. I know it was so in my own case—I think it was so with most people old enough to remember anything of the last war. The thing had happened again that we hoped could never happen again, the crack in civilization, the ultimate evil, war. Not just war in Ethiopia, war in Spain, war in Finland—minor wars where we could sympathize appropriately with the losing side and form committees for their relief while they were being defeated—but the big war that had lain like a black cloud at the back of our thinking for years.

Still, it was Europe's war. It couldn't touch us, except in our minds and our sympathies. And the right side would win, of course. The Nazi tanks were jaloppies and the Nazi planes *ersatz*. Mussolini was a sensible man, for a dictator, and wouldn't risk his brand-new empire in anything serious. Stalin was playing a deep game and the Nazi-Communist pact was really a triumph for socialism and peace. Do you recognize any of those phrases? They were all said, and doubtless believed. They may seem a long way away, now. But they were all said.

So, after the crushing of Poland, like Britain and France themselves we passed into a strange lull of mind. I recall the phrase "phony war," spoken by supposedly responsible American statesmen. I remember a young and ardent Leftist explaining to me earnestly that it was all a put-up job on the part of the capitalist democracies. They weren't fighting because they didn't mean to fight till they could turn on Russia. The historian of the future—writing perhaps from a comfortable igloo at the North Pole—will find nothing more singular, ominous and strange than that strange lull.

Then came May, the breaking of France, the wiping out of five free nations.

And, with a shock like that of winter in August, we began to realize as a nation—not just the government, not just a few individuals, but as a nation—that the totalitarians meant precisely what they said. They hated democracy and meant to wipe it out. They set war as the highest human activity and waged it with total force. They were ready and capable in using every means—words, thoughts, ideas as well as tanks, guns, dive-bombers. They divided from within, then struck from without. And all this was part of a single and consistent theory—a new theory of the State, a new theory of the state of man. They went back to master and helot, to lord and serf—back beyond the Middle Ages—beyond the Roman Empire—back to Sparta. Only this Sparta was not a small city-state but a vast and complex mechanism—the ultimate machine. In the driver's seat sat a little man, to be worshipped as a god.

Painfully, slowly, bloodily, over centuries, democracy had struggled into being. Painfully, slowly, bloodily, it had struggled into being here. It was not handed down from on high; the struggle of free men made it. It did not depend upon revelation; it said, "We hold these truths to be self-evident." It chose—and rejected—its effective political rulers. It believed men could govern themselves.

We had lived in it all our lives and we knew its mistakes and abuses. Sometimes these loomed very large to us. But, even when they loomed very large, we knew there was a residuum left—an idea and a way of life that was neither mistaken nor abused. That was the part of the iceberg under water—the part that did not show on the surface. It is curious to look back, historically, and see what a high price was paid, by quite ordinary men, in endurance, shock and sacrifice for some of the average liberties we had always taken for granted.

Now, slowly to some, to others more sharply, one fact is borne in upon us—that democracy is not of itself and necessarily a self-perpetuating thing. A tree may grow for many years but a tree can be cut down. My father may build a house—I may let it rot and ruin. The past may give us liberty. It cannot guarantee us liberty. There are generations that live and die without seeing their freedom menaced or their deep beliefs put to the question. Ours is not such a generation. If we had thought so once, we can think so no longer. The writing on the wall of the world is too plain.

Democracy can be betrayed. Democracy can be chained. Democracy can be killed.

Those are the trite and iron facts of the case, and the sooner we accept them the better. For we have time—still—to examine the hows and the whys. We have time—still—to look into our own minds and see which of our old beliefs, prejudices, convictions still seem to hold water. We have time—still—to learn certain lessons from the easy-going, the sincere and the deluded who shut their eyes to tomorrow because they did not like the look of it. We have time—still—to learn even from the defeatists and their defeat.

To do so—to try to do so—is not a mental exercise. It is a vital necessity. Behind the armed force of any nation lies the will and purpose of that nation. That will and purpose may be dominated and imposed upon the whole nation by a small and ruthless minority. That is not our way and it never has been our way. It never will be our way while we stand ready to look at facts and judge them. We have faced hard facts in the past. We can do so again.

We must do so because total war and the total propaganda which is one great instrument of that war can only be met by total defense. And the war in Europe is a war of minds and ideas as well as a war of bombs and shell. Should war ever come to America, it will be a war of minds and ideas as well as a war of bombs and shell. We have seen one great nation fall because it had confidence in a string of fortifications—and yet, when the pinch came, no confidence in itself. We have seen both over-confidence and defeatism produce disaster. Both are dangers, to be thought of as dangers, but to be thought of realistically and without hysteria. We are supposed to be a quick-moving and nervously emotional people. But we can take the long grind, once we know what it's about.

We can take it if we want—that is always the choice. We can order vast armaments and still be unprepared. Unless we believe that democracy is worth saving, worth defending, we will not be able to defend it. And then indeed we shall enter a waste land—more waste and more dread than the disillusion of the poet can compass—the land of the night of the mind where force and the cruel myths of force rule unchecked and unhindered over their shadowy slaves.

2

This book is neither a formal history of the past few years nor a blueprint for the future. It is an adventure in thinking by six very different minds—an attempt to clarify certain pressing American issues. I note with interest that the five principal contributors represent by birth four different States of the Union and one foreign country—a rather American average. And, if you happened to go into the racial strains of the various writers here, including my own, you would find most, though not all of the various stocks that have settled this continent—French, Spanish, English, German, Dutch, Irish, Scotch-Irish. That seems rather American, too.

Erika Mann, daughter of Thomas Mann, was a successful

actress, author and director in post-war Republican Germany. She was a liberal pacifist, chiefly interested in the arts. She is a refugee and an exile, about to take out her first papers as a citizen of the United States. As she describes herself and her friends of those former days, in the middle section of her article, the portrait has certain implications that I find it hard to dismiss. She is talking of Germany—I have never been to Germany. But I know the sort of talk that she reproduces—I have heard plenty in New York. A few of the phrases differ but that is all. If Miss Mann spoke from personal grievance, that indeed would be another matter. But, oddly enough, her chief concern is not with herself, though she uses herself as a case-history. Her chief concern seems to be with certain very practical things—the essential defenses of freedom against the forces that would destroy it. She has not written a scare-story or a shilling-shocker of the sort with which we are all familiar. She has been candid about herself, about her former country and about her new one. And perhaps for that very reason her grave candor may be heard.

McGeorge Bundy, a very recent graduate of Yale, Class Day Orator, Phi Beta Kappa and Sigma Xi, head of the Liberal Party in the Student Union and the winner of innumerable prizes from his earnest University, belongs to the most bitterly attacked and hotly discussed generation in twenty years—the generation now or recently in the colleges. We have had heated attack and equally heated defense—we have had very little of what that generation itself has to say. Mr. Bundy states it. It is a personal viewpoint. It is not shared by all his contemporaries. But in its direct lucidity, its anxiety to be fair and its cool yet resilient temper, it seems to me an unusual and significant document. I doubt if anyone in the colleges before or during the crisis of 1917 could have produced so clear and yet resolute a summing-up. I doubt it because I remember, with occasional but painful acuteness, what was then being written.

The third voice, William L. White's, has a different timbre. Ex-member of the Kansas State Legislature, part-publisher of the Emporia *Gazette,* newspaperman, foreign correspondent for forty American daily newspapers, White has his own tale to tell —the tale of a skilled and intelligent newspaperman, working in Europe and putting down what he saw, but thinking in American terms. His frame of reference is neither that of the Eastern seaboard nor that of the cosmopolitanism of art but directly and avowedly that of the Middle West. That is what he keeps going back to—that is where, if you will notice, most of his similes start. Yet, though in a different way from Miss Mann, he is no less concerned by what he has seen.

Garrett Underhill, grandson of one general and nephew of another, comes legitimately by his precise and technical interest in military and naval affairs. On the staff of *Life* he has devoted a good deal of his time to debunking war inaccuracies in picture or print. Younger than most of our military commentators, he is by no means the least brilliant. He brings a fresh point of view to the problems of national defense.

The last contributor, Walter Millis, is already well known, not only as an analyst of war but of the human motives and the human mistakes that lead to it. His two books, *The Martial Spirit* and *The Road to War* have deeply influenced contemporary opinion—particularly the opinion of Mr. Bundy's generation. In his present article, with the same unsparing frankness that distinguished those two books, he analyzes why certain remedies against another war failed, why certain policies proved futile and where, in his opinion, we must stand today. And the demonstration is exact, though not without hope.

3

So much for the book itself. It is both factual and personal. In writing it, the contributors have not spared themselves. They have not pretended to be all-wise and they have avoided the rhetoric of calamity and hysteria. Yet they all acknowledge a crisis and a crisis that must be met—by mind and thought and intelligence as well as by deed and act—not next week, not tomorrow, but now. More than that, they acknowledge a faith—a faith implicit in their very warnings—that with open eyes to the truth, by knowledge and faith and strength, free men working together can maintain the great shape of democracy, the great, daring and limitless dream of man's free mind. In that faith I share, and wholly. But the hands of the clock are hurrying as I write.

II

DON'T MAKE THE SAME MISTAKES

Erika Mann

II

DON'T MAKE THE SAME MISTAKES

I

CONVERSATION ON THE TRAIN

THE YOUNG American who made the trip from Chicago to Los Angeles on the same train as I, was about twenty-one years old. Wherever I saw him, in the club car, in the dining car, in the observation car, he was reading. He had brought with him a whole stack of newspapers and magazines, but apparently did not strictly adhere to any particular political viewpoint. He read the *Nation* and the *New Republic* with the same detached interest which he gave to the Hearst papers and the *Saturday Evening Post.* He had dark hair, and bright, friendly eyes; every now and then two thoughtful lines appeared between his thick brows.

On the second day of going through the desert, we started to talk. He had noticed the European stickers on my luggage as he strolled by my seat. "You come from over there?" he asked—and shortly a conversation on the political situation was in full swing. He asked me many questions, that well-read young man, and his interest in my answers was sincere. Of course, he had never been "over there"—but he knew and loved French paintings and literature, and German music; he had relatives in England.

"So many great, beautiful and stimulating things have come from Europe," he said, "even in those last few years. That's why the collapse of worlds which is going on there now comes as such a surprise and is so impossible to explain."

"I know what you're going to say," he kept me from interrupting with a motion of his hand, "but that is really no explanation. You want to say that Germany lost the war and therefore had to wage a war of revenge; you want to say that the victorious democracies were satiated, tired and worn; that they had bad consciences because of the Versailles Treaty; that they were afraid of Russia and because of that fear alone would do nothing against the Nazis; that the Nazis proceeded step by step and that each single step appeared bearable to the democracies—until ultimately came the sum of all the steps which was unbearable. That's what you were going to say, isn't it?"

I shook my head. "Not exactly," I said. "But what *you* said is absolutely true. Only it seems to me little is gained by the diagnosis of a disease if you can't at the same time propose a cure. Perhaps the disease is incurable, once you catch it. But as long as it still rages only in the immediate neighborhood, means must be found to prevent its spreading."

The young man glanced up sharply. "In the neighborhood? Is Europe our neighborhood? Isn't the Atlantic Ocean between us? But even without the ocean; some people are immune to certain diseases. I believe that we in America are immune to Nazism. First of all, we have not lost a war; second, our democracy is not of yesterday, just as Hitler's dictatorship is not of yesterday. The German tradition . . ."

Now it was I who stopped him. "I know what you are going to say." No doubt: he was going to conjure up Washington and Lincoln and contrast them with Frederick the Great and Bismarck. He was going to say that anti-humanitarian tendencies have always existed in Germany; yes, that all "great men" in German history have been anti-humanitarian, anti-democratic, "authoritarian" and militaristic. But in America, freedom was at home. America was immune to any disease whose first symptom was the destruction of freedom.

I said, "Wait a moment. And let's take one thing at a time. In the first place, as regards your ocean—the other day somebody called it the Maginot Ocean, and that's not such a bad name."

The young man sat up. "Maginot Ocean?"

I nodded affirmation. "Of course," I continued, "there's a great difference. You didn't dig the ocean yourselves and fill it with water. You received it as a gift from God. But otherwise, the situation's pretty much the same. For, in the first place, until recently, you relied entirely on your ocean just as the French relied up to the last moment on their Maginot Line. And, in the second place, it is not inconceivable that you might get the same sorry surprise as the French. The 'Maginot psychology' is ruinous. There is no security for anyone who wants nothing but security."

"France!" the young man said, and looked at me angrily, "France broke down because fascist and communist treachery within the country made its defense impossible—and not because of your 'Maginot psychology.' That couldn't happen to us. We *are* immune to some things."

I said, "One and the same disease can have different causes. I'll grant you that lack of democratic traditions and lack of love of freedom will hardly be the cause here. It's more likely that the very overabundance of your freedom could become dangerous to you. Moreover, isn't it true that your inclination to standardization and uniformity, your delight in spreading of half-true slogans, in simplification and popularization of ideas, might also become dangerous? Isn't it true that you have a certain predilection for all kinds of religions, sects, faith-healers, radio priests; further, you are virtually the inventors of modern 'propaganda'? Your racial psychology, the unsolved Negro question—they could also become the breeding place of the disease."

The young man looked out of the window. "And unemployment," he said without turning his gaze away from the desert, "and lynch law—the unpunished acts of violence that run through our history. And the fact that we worship success. . . ."

He looked like a child who has been scolded and knows why, but remains nevertheless stubborn.

"For we do worship success," he declared and his head went up, "we admire success. We think it's a goal in itself. I don't think that a lot of Americans like Hitler. But many, very many, admire him because of his success."

The steward came bringing a telegram to the young man. He asked politely if he might read it. "From England," he then explained. "My sister would like to come over here with her little children. It is getting too hot for them there since the crackup of France."

There they were again—European politics. Even the little interruption—the steward with his tray—did not lead us away from them.

"The crackup of France," the young man repeated. "I still can't believe it. And no 'explanation' can make it understandable. It is exactly as if someone very close to you suddenly died and every morning you woke up and simply refused to believe it. How could it have happened?" he asked and looked intently at me. "How could it happen so terribly fast?"

I said, "The resistance did not function."

"Obviously not," he said and smiled bitterly.

I said, "But you have to know what that means: 'the resistance did not function.' It means more, much more than military failure and political treachery in the last hour. It means a general breakdown of all forces of resistance and morale—of all the mental and psychological forces. And this general breakdown did not begin just on September 3, 1939. It was apparent as early as the winter of 1918–1919, at about the same time as we in Republican Germany began noting our first mistakes. But, dear God, how much others could still learn from our failure!"

The young man made a little sound expressing his disagreement. At this moment, his face was interested, child-like, and at the same time a little out of sympathy, a little supercilious, and removed; he held his head cocked on the side, like a hunting dog, listening to distant, disturbing noises.

"Others?" he finally asked. "Does that mean us? Do you seriously believe that we here could learn much from the destruction of worlds over there, beyond the 'Maginot Ocean'?"

I said, "I am thirty-four years old." This was no answer and so the young man waited patiently to see if I had anything more sensible to say. I continued, "Thirty-four years. That means I am twelve or thirteen years older than you are. But in reality, there is much more between us than those thirteen years. Because first"—and my smile asked his forgiveness for the platitude which I was about to bring forth—"first, I come from a much, much older continent. Young Americans are younger than young Europeans. Second, these twelve or thirteen years are more today than they were, let's say, during the last century. And third, I must repeat it, we have made so many mistakes during that time and we have seen so many mistakes with our very eyes that we are older by decades. Sometimes we feel like ancients who see generation after generation pass before them, each one refusing viciously to learn from what the preceding has experienced and suffered."

The young man shrugged his shoulders. "There isn't much we can learn from you," he said. "Europe is not America and our conditions here are basically different from yours."

"But that's exactly what *we* said," I answered heatedly. "Germany is not Italy, we used to say, and we were quite right. Yet the horror came upon us too, despite the difference in our conditions. How different were the French conditions from ours. And yet France is lost and might have saved herself had she but wanted to learn from our mistakes. The final causes of failure are the same in all democracies; and they will be the same with you."

"Excuse me," the young man retorted, and his bright eyes took on a grey-black color. "We have not failed yet. And may I say, there is no indication that we will fail in the near future."

I was remorseful, but I continued steadfastly. "No," I said, "you have not failed yet. But will you not fail eventually? The similarity between your situation today and the German situation at the beginning of the thirties is striking, and terribly disturbing. By the way, it was the same in France and England. There, between 1933 and 1939, all the mistakes we made prior to 1933 were repeated. You will not believe," I added, and noticed that my tone was a little too intense, "you can't imagine how painful it is gradually to discover that no country, no nation, no youth has wanted to draw a lesson from our dreadful example."

"Perhaps," the young man said coolly, "but one shouldn't

demand too much. You can't expect us to get wisdom from the spectacle of other people's misfortunes and to learn from their mistakes. We want to make our own mistakes and, if need be, learn from them."

He crushed out his cigarette with a quick, short motion of his hand. It was as if he were looking forward with grim joy to all the mistakes he was going to make in the near future.

"Besides," he added stubbornly, "the whole thing 'over there' is really none of our business. We have other worries. We have, for instance, our great and pressing worry about the survival of our democracy and our social achievements. For our democracy," he emphasized and looked at me pointedly, "is really in danger. But not because of the Maginot Ocean and the attractive successes of Mr. Hitler—or rather, only indirectly because of them. While we are making all efforts to become 'strong' so that at some later time our 'resistance' may function, we are in danger of a voluntary renunciation of those things in the defense of which that 'resistance' is built. Civil liberties!" he exclaimed. "Freedom of speech! The rights of labor! The two-party system. Why, we are facing dangers from the 'inside' which might easily prove fatal because of the wanton exaggeration by certain interested groups of the dangers from the 'outside.'"

I caught myself nodding as if hearing in a dream an old, somewhat worn melody. "Oh, yes," I murmured, "of course. Of course."

But the young man was undaunted. "We have grave and numerous problems here," he continued. "And no side-tracking, no 'preparedness program,' no 'state of national emergency' can invalidate them. We've got to solve these problems of ours, no matter what goes on in Europe. I will admit that we would prefer England to continue running the show over there. We criticize England a lot, you know that. But somehow a certain way of living together has grown between us and the Empire. But if England fails and Germany takes over the whole darned show, then it's not our fault and we will have to find a new way of living together—with Germany. After all, these things work themselves out and history goes on."

He interrupted himself. "It's funny," he said, "but I talk differently, too. Sometimes, it seems to me that we ought to do everything, *everything* to prevent a victory by Hitler. At such times I think that there's probably no way of living together with the thing called Nazi Germany, the thing called Nazi Europe; and no life in what would be called Nazi World. But in the end, I ask myself what does it mean 'to do everything'? And what for Heaven's sake are we to do? What can we do to prevent a Nazi victory? It seems to me," he said and smiled charmingly, "that you are right and our resistance does not function in the right manner."

I nodded to him as if he had said something quite encouraging. "You see," I said, "now we are entirely agreed. But please don't believe that your domestic worries of today have no resemblance to Germany's worries of yesteryear and Europe's of yesterday. I can see among them many problems which absorbed us in Germany ten years ago. It is easy to recognize them. They have familiar faces and they have never been far out of my sight. I saw them in every European democracy, all of them, and with no changes after 1933. But over there, no one wanted to admit, either, that they were beset by the very same ancient problems which beset us. 'These are new problems,' people insisted, 'and therefore we can learn nothing from the inadequate ways in which you dealt with your old problems.' "

The young man said, "If only the things which we want to defend had progressed a little further, were just a little closer to perfection, then the resistance would be better and more perfect. We are a little skeptical, you know. We've lost a bit of our faith in the 'values' for which we are supposed to fight."

"A little skeptical?" I exclaimed. "Only a little? But you are *very* skeptical. Down deep, you are skeptical, and even in that you resemble us like peas in a pod. Do please remember that the disillusionment of youth after the first World War was identical in all countries. Only Germany had lost the war; that is true. But we all lost the peace. You, as well as we. The deep and discouraging disappointment in the fact that the world was by no means safe for democracy was common to all of us."

"I know that," the young man returned somewhat impatiently, "but outside that, try as I may, I don't see much that we have in common. Please tell me where *is* the similarity between Germany of 1931, England and France of 1938, and America of 1940? Where are the common sources of failure? What did you Europeans do to get yourself into such a mess? And what are we supposed to do to stay out of it? Could you tell me that, as briefly and easily as possible?"

I had a pencil in my hand and drew little figures on the back of the telegram from England which lay between us on the table. The young man watched. I had drawn a big "D" and a swastika and a hammer and sickle. "D for democracy," I explained.

"Briefly and easily?" I then asked, feeling somewhat apprehensive. "Let me see. I am to give you a report of all our mistakes, faults, and crimes of omission. Furthermore, I am supposed to show you that (a) Europe, instead of avoiding them, has copied all mistakes, faults and crimes of omission from

Republican Germany. And that (b) America is also not far from repetition of those same mistakes, faults and crimes of omission. I am to explain why 'resistance' did not function, first in Germany, then in the rest of Europe, and finally, foretell whether it will not function here either. Is that the idea?"

"Pretty much so," the young man answered, "except for the last part. Not foretell. You can't foretell. Partially because you don't know us, because you haven't had the opportunity to know America intimately enough yet to interpret our actions and reactions exactly. Please—just the report. I'll pick out of it what seems to me convincing and true."

It sounded a little supercilious as he said it. He was like the rich man who listens to one who squandered his fortune explain what it's like to be poor but never realizes that, after all, his own wealth may not last forever. Nevertheless, I liked him. His superciliousness, I thought, comes from great reserves of power; it comes from a feeling of security which is inborn and has nothing to do with the "Maginot Ocean."

I was still doodling. "It is late," I said, "and the task assigned the 'pupil' is anything but easy. I'd like to put my thoughts in order and not rush them. Do you know what?" I suddenly said, and put my pencil determinedly in my pocket, "I'll write it down for you. I'll try to solve the problem on paper. If I scribble all day tomorrow, I'll finish it, that horrifying picture. Then, before getting off the train, I'll make you a parting present of it."

With a little bow, the young man accepted the offer.

Outside the window, the desert stretched endlessly. "Our country is big," the young man said and with his slightly skeptical smile, he added, "or isn't that true either, and perhaps tomorrow you will write that our country is small, poor and weak?"

To that I gave no answer. I only said, "I will make the greatest effort to be thorough and sincere and I shall attempt to tell nothing but the truth."

"The truth," the young man said slowly, "is complex and can be looked at from so many sides. Isn't there a subjective and objective truth? And what was true over there—must it also hold true here?"

Suddenly he seemed older than I was. That came from the weary callousness in which he now took refuge. He pretended that I was trying to concern him with remote things, which, although perhaps interesting, possessed no reality for him whatever.

"At any rate, I'm sure what you're going to write will be very interesting," he said. "Perhaps I'll learn something from it all —for later on."

I thought: For later on? My God, it is later than we think. And how easily could it happen here—how easily, here again, it might be too late! But I said nothing.

The young man suddenly leaned toward me across the table and looked into my face wide-eyed, serious, his expression questioning.

"There is only one more thing I would like to know before you start," he said. "With all your warnings, and parallels, are you concerned about Europe—or about this country? What I mean is would you like us to 'save' Europe, or are you thinking primarily of America?"

"I will write it down for you," I repeated. Again that was no answer, but he seemed satisfied by the tone of my voice.

"All right," he said. "How about a drink?"

2

REPORT TO A TRIP COMPANION

1. Symptoms of Decay

This task which I am attempting is not easy. Now that I sit alone before my window, and this country in its undeniable grandeur and strangeness rolls by, it seems to me it would have been much easier to *talk* to that young man. Certainly, his retorts often confused me. Not because he held a different opinion, but because on the really decisive points, he did not seem to have any opinion at all; and because he believed truth to be so many-sided and bottomless, that it would be a futile undertaking for us even to attempt to get to a bottom.

But there is only one truth, as there is only one morale, the morale of the individual. And, with all due honor to the richness of the nuances, "good" and "evil," "right" and "wrong" do exist. The absolute exists. That is what he should know, that young man. That is what he must believe.

Can I expect him to take *my* word for it? Of course not! Do I want to preach to him? Not that either. I am not smarter than he, and probably less self-assured. But I have had more experience. And the fact that I know the symptoms of the disease which endangers all our lives gives me, perhaps, the right to speak.

In my talk with him, I understated the importance of "diagnosis." Without diagnosis, there is no cure. Nor is there prevention without diagnosis.

But what constitutes the disease? Fascism, Nazism, dictatorship, defeat? No! Because they already are Death. The "disease"—that is the inability of the body to resist Death. The decay of the organism, the breakdown of resistance, that is the disease.

Europe was ailing after the first World War. But although the disease appeared only sporadically, and not all of its symptoms were obvious everywhere at the same time, it nevertheless attacked all countries alike.

Incidentally, many of the symptoms in France were exactly the same as those in Germany and Italy. Even England and America were not spared.

After the War, there was deep disillusionment everywhere, and a "nihilism" created by this disillusionment. Everywhere was the feeling of having been cheated. Everywhere youth sought compensation for the privations and hardships of the "great times" just passed. Everywhere they plunged into violent pleasures and excesses. New and wild music coming from America was an intoxicant. But it was no longer an intoxication for a "cause" (as for instance, the patriotic intoxication for the "fatherland"). It was intoxication, in general, admittedly and emphatically for no cause at all. In order to intensify it, all methods were permissible; music and alcohol, marihuana, morphine and cocaine. In the back rooms of Berlin's night clubs, narcotic poisons were sold just as in the harbor saloons of Marseilles or in the night clubs of Harlem, New York.

The "inflation"—devaluation of all values which took place in Germany and France alike—had its moral equivalent in all countries of the world after the War. Everywhere, what had been valid yesterday was no longer so. One had been cheated by this War. Too long had its laws been obeyed in good faith. All that was over. Of a sudden, everything and anything was permissible.

Even in art, everything and anything was permissible. Expressionism paid no attention to form at all. It shouted, it raged, it banged the cymbals like a jazz orchestra. Authority, Law, had lost out. All expressions of that time were exciting and at the same time cynically aggressive. In Germany, a whole literature came into existence dealing with father-murder. But "Father" was also nothing else but the personified symbol of authority and law which had lost out.

Sigmund Freud and psychoanalysis gave a scientific explanation resulting even in a glorification of this psychological process. The "unconscious" and the "repressions," the "complexes" and "traumas" were the craze, and openly acknowledged by all the world.

Girls wore skirts which showed their knees, if they did not prefer to dress like young men in the evening. It was considered chic to be erotically perverted, to have just some slight peculiarity. But most of all, it was considered foolish, if not indecent, to believe in something, in *anything*. "We have been so terribly cheated by this War," young men all over the world cried out. "From now on, we just won't believe in anything." And they were proud of their chic nihilism.

That was the atmosphere of the twenties and it is important to recall that it was the same everywhere and not only in defeated Germany.

The inordinate love of pleasure on the part of the young, life-thirsty, post-war generation, purposely overlooked the greatness of the tasks before it. And the generation of parents seemed exhausted and weary from fighting. Neither did the victorious democracies see that nothing decisive was gained by the destruction of Imperial Germany, that nothing was "settled"—nor did Republican Germany wish to recognize how weak the legs were on which she stood. Here, as well as there, the reins were slackening. The wounds which the War had inflicted upon the peoples were deep. Where neither apathy nor weariness ruled, wound-fever broke out. But the hectic and super-animated activity which it created was misunderstood. Because in some places there was feverish energy, it was thought that productive regeneration was in full force. Even the restless and curious lust for travelling which came upon us at that time was looked upon as a "new will for understanding" among the nations.

Everywhere, there were meetings, congresses, international gatherings. The students, the writers, the women's organizations got together in the capitals of Europe. By the thousands, Americans flocked to Paris where they met with thousands of Germans, Russians, Italians, Englishmen. They held discussions, ate, drank—they enjoyed peace and freedom. But did they actually learn to know each other? Did they have a living insight into each other's problems? Did they try jointly to solve those problems? Hardly. Everything was most interesting, most stimulating and pleasant. On the speakers' platforms, from speakers' tables, people were seized by fever when they spoke of the League of Nations, as "the new and impregnable fortress of peace." But it was unfortified, this fortress. America had refused to become a part of its defense and Europe alone did not have the power to defend it. The "fortress of freedom" had neither power nor respect. If it had not existed at all, it would have been much better. The deceptive and dangerous idea of security stood on a fake foundation.

The deceptive and dangerous idea of security! Of that first and foremost, I must speak to that American young man. Because that was what, in infinite forms, thrust Europe into disaster, and that is what might become dangerous to America.

The democracies went to war "to make the world safe for democracy." Now after they had won it, their thought at first was that the world was *automatically* safe for democracy. That was dangerous, and before long, it became obvious that, at the least, it was not right.

There *was* no security and security was all that was wanted. But instead of realizing that peace was indivisible and that the security for all was in the interest of all, each single country insisted only on that which it thought best for its own protection. The attitude of the individual countries was absolutely asocial. England's concept of English security, the balance-of-power idea, robbed France of the chance to assume the leadership in Europe. And France, this highly civilized country, should have been leading in the interest of security for all. But England thought herself safe only if there was *no* leader. On the other hand, France gladly renounced such a role. In order to be absolutely secure, France thought, one must not "lead." "Leading" creates enemies, and France, which wanted no enemies, was as if hypnotized by the idea of "sécurité." All one had to do to obtain security, absolute security, was to build impregnable fortifications and pay no attention to what was going on outside these fortifications.

"Collective security?" "Indivisibility of peace?" "European Concert of Powers?" No one was really serious about it. They wanted to protect themselves and only themselves. And thus they brought danger on themselves and others.

The "Maginot psychology" of which we had spoken yesterday, that young American and I, was general.

The mental Maginot Line which might have been able to safeguard the continent, the world, remained non-existent. The moral fortifications of the earth which alone held prospects of security were never built.

These are general truths; undeniable, it seems to me. Even my partner of yesterday would not have denied them. Perhaps he will utter his little mocking laugh when he reads this and say "That's obvious." But he should remember that these truths, general and obvious as they may be, form the basis of our situation today. I will summarize them here briefly.

1. The world was disappointed, skeptical and discouraged after the War. It was weakened and bled out and unable to cope with the enormous tasks which presented themselves.

2. A certain hectic stimulation and activity which was felt was no symptom of recuperation. It was feverish and did not serve for the regeneration of the wounded organism but rather for its destruction.

3. The skeptic and discouraged, but at the same time feverish, world had in its weakness no other thought but that of security. But as it was unable to create real security, real appeasement, because of the short-sighted egotism of all concerned—lack of spiritual and moral foundations—it fell under the spell of the "Maginot-Psychologie," the fatal "Maginot mistake."

How did that develop—in Germany and elsewhere? Did we have no eyes for what was coming? Why did our "resistance" fail so completely?

I had promised the young man to give him a picture of our mistakes and our omissions. And I had contended that he would recognize some of our mistakes and omissions in his own country.

Well, then, what was it like? What was our situation during that period "before Hitler"? And, inasmuch as it is I who have to deliver this report, what, more particularly, was *my* situation?

2. A Non-Political Actress

I wanted to become an actress. I was set on it body and soul. It was my good fortune to live in our capital and have the privilege of going to Max Reinhardt's school. Berlin was the best, the most stimulating theatrical city on the continent.

When I finished studying, I acted in plays by Shaw, Strindberg, Pirandello and the modern German authors. Nothing was so important to me as the lines which I had to say and the steps and motions which I had to make. Despite an intense desire for pleasure, the passion with which I clung to my profession gave me a certain earnestness. Furthermore, the contents of those plays forced one to think about all possible social and political problems. Of course, I was a "pacifist." War was shameful; war was impossible—there would never be war again. I was convinced of that without doing anything on my part to work for peace. Such things were decidedly none of my business. I loved the anti-war poems by Werfel and Ernst Toller. I learned them by heart and gave evening recitals of them. Young intellectuals and my friends from the "Youth Movement" were in the audience, and applauded. To the "Youth Movement" belonged the many young Germans who wanted to go "back to nature" because they despised the pleasure-seeking cynicism of the big cities. The "Youth Movement" rejected even bourgeois clothes; they wore loose frocks and sandals and spent their nights around campfires instead of the night clubs of Berlin filled with smoke and jazz. Girls slept with boys; boys with boys; girls with girls; teachers (who called themselves "comrades") with male and female pupils. For the Youth Movement, too, had thrown overboard all traditional laws; neither authority nor the family should have voice in the counsel of the young. But the young ones were free to do anything. The individualism of the Youth Movement, their intoxication with Nature and their anti-bourgeois pathos had a different character than our anti-political and non-political callousness. But by no means was it less asocial or more conscious of any responsibility.

Yet with the growing misery, poverty and unemployment in Germany, even we could not avoid occasionally thinking about "politics" which, however, we always ended up by deciding was none of our business. The ruling middle parties were worried by the radical parties on the "Right" as well as those on the "Left." Especially did the Nazis appear to be growing dangerously in force and momentum. That caused the middle parties to create some few technical measures of safety (Maginot psychology). But it did not make them put up a forceful, spiritually and morally unassailable, united and fighting defense front against the aggressor.

In the early summer of 1931, I was asked to recite a poem at a meeting. The great French woman pacifist, Marcelle Capi, was scheduled to speak. I was to recite some lines, pacifistic in character.

The great hall was filled to capacity. Women made up most of the audience. But there were also the "intellectuals" with horn-rimmed glasses, the young people of the Youth Movement in frocks and sandals, and, in smaller number, representatives of the "progressive students."

Marcelle Capi spoke well and convincingly. The audience was impressed with the material she presented to prove that the peace which we all wanted was not yet secure; it was still in danger. The international armament industry was at work to endanger it. But, on the other hand, such a meeting as this was proof that "we" were at our posts and were not going to let ourselves be cheated for the second time.

While waiting in the wings for my entrance, I was thinking: Strange—all she says is true and I agree with her. Why then doesn't she move me, why doesn't she really inspire me? She is logical, sincere, and intelligent. The things she defends are certainly worth defending. But obviously, "defending" in itself is not a grateful task. In the first place, it is thankless to defend something which admittedly is imperfect and defective. One should try to better it in order to make oneself able to defend it with greater force. One should be more constructive, and more militant, and perhaps then one could arouse more enthusiasm.

Marcelle Capi had finished. The audience applauded, politely and respectfully. But I was not uplifted by her message even at the end. She had sounded a warning, that was true. She had given us food for thought about the existence of a danger; but how to fight it, she did not tell us. Besides, I was not even sure that she did not underestimate the danger. Was it only the "criminal interests," only the "armament industry" which did not want this peace any more? Or was it not rather that all those who were badly off did not want it? That all the dissatisfied, disappointed and rebellious in our country wanted something new, something else than *this* peace?

My name was announced on the stage. I made my entrance.

Marcelle Capi had spoken in French. That had erected some kind of barrier between her and her German-speaking audience. I was at an advantage, for I was to recite a German poem. I felt that my voice sounded convincing and I tried to give it some militant quality while I spoke those pacifistic lines.

But after a short time, there was evidence of restiveness in the audience. A few youngsters in the gallery booed and yelled. Women in the orchestra hissed for quiet. I was not daunted and kept on reciting, although the noise disturbed me considerably. Then came a greater, more ominous noise from outside. Apparently, a fight was going on there between the ushers and a group of people demanding admittance.

The doors were flung open. Thirty or forty young men in brown shirts of the National Socialist Storm Troops rushed into the hall.

I stopped, waiting until the young men should find their places and keep quiet. Efficiently, and skillfully, they spread out all over the hall.

I continued. "War"—that was the gist of my words—"is unworthy of humanity. It is shameful and a crime. . . ."

One of the bownshirted lads had come close to the stage. To this day I can still see his face distorted by hate, with the narrow forehead upon which fell a greasy lock of blond hair.

"Do you hear that?" he suddenly shouted and turned to the audience. "Did you hear how she insulted our glorious fighters? Our soldiers are 'criminals,' she said, and 'it is a shame to die for the fatherland.' . . . You are a criminal, yourself!" he shouted and made a move as if to attack me. "Jewish traitress! International agitator! Gets up here together with a Frenchwoman. . . ." he yelled and there was a chasm of hateful contempt in the word "Frenchwoman"—"with the eternal enemy of our nation. . . ."

Soothingly and admonishingly, I raised my hands. I spoke, I argued. "I did not insult the soldiers," I cried. "What are you talking about? Besides, this poem is not even by me. Please listen," I begged.

But the noise was too great; I could not surmount it. The men in the galleries began to fight. Six or eight of them beat up one young man, apparently a Jewish intellectual. I do not believe that he, on his part, had done anything to irritate them. They just didn't like his face. Or perhaps he had applauded after Marcelle Capi had finished.

In the hall, everything became a mad scramble. The Storm Troopers attacked the audience with chairs, shouting themselves into paroxysms of anger and fury. Their numbers seemed to grow. Part of our audience took sides with the attackers whose conviction they could not possibly have shared. They were simply infected with the mass madness. Women fled, crying. Some of the "progressive students" defended themselves effectively. Fist fights sprang up everywhere in the hall. The chairman shouted "Police, police!" But there were no police around.

Finally, the hall emptied almost entirely. On the street, the still fighting groups were finally dissolved by police. Gradually the noise subsided. Peace—in the defense of which this meeting was called—was restored. The meeting, however, was over and finished. It was disrupted by those who branded as "traitors of the fatherland" those who spoke of "peace." To them, every Frenchman was a hereditary enemy.

I remained alone in the darkened hall. It was not safe to venture outside too early. First, the streets had to be cleared.

What madness! Nothing could have been less provocative than this meeting, less provocative than the poem which I had begun to recite. Was it possible that those men hated peace? Did they want war? I could not believe it. I rather got the impression that they were desperate and that they *hated*—no matter whom or what! But why, of all things, did they choose us and our harmless meeting? That could be no coincidence. And why did they lie so? It was impossible that they misunderstood what I said.

Not with one word had I insulted the soldiers. They had called me "Jewish traitress." They knew that I was not a Jewess and that I had said nothing traitorous. Was it impossible to talk sense to them? Was it hopeless to attempt to convince them?

To a halfway reasonable and sensible person, it is an uncanny, yes, even an unbelievable experience to meet beings entirely unapproachable by arguments of logic and reason. I thought: If I had said to those men "The sea is deep," or "The snow, white," they would have replied, with all the hatred and distortion of their fury, that I was an internationalistic liar; that the sea was shallow and the snow brown.

And while cold shudders ran down my spine, I knew: Many of those in the hall believed the furious insistence of those Nazis, nonsensical as it was.

Those men, as a whole, whatever the reason might be, possessed the passion of madness. My audience, as a whole, whatever the reason might be, was disunited, skeptical, prone to experiments, and, moreover, easily frightened by such men who, in contrast to them (the audience) knew exactly what they wanted. Of my audience, some would have fallen under the spell of the fanaticism with which those Nazis affirmed their nonsense. Others might have known that what they heard was nonsense, but they would have wavered as to whether in certain moments even nonsense did not have its basic reasons. Again, others would have simply been afraid to contradict. All in all, I was by no means certain whether in face of such aggressive madness, I would have been able to hold my place even with such a contention as that the sea was deep and the snow white.

I swayed. I was sick at the pit of my stomach.

A few days of bewilderment and restlessness followed. The fact that I found myself insulted in the *Völkischer Beobachter* as a "flatfooted peace hyena" hardly surprised me. Even the fact that the theatre at which I had been engaged for the coming summer festival tore up my contract, I bore with equanimity.

The Nazi Party, the director explained to me, stutteringly, had threatened him with a general boycott of all performances should I appear even in one. Of course, I would understand that he had to yield. I understood. "The sea is shallow," I said, "and the snow is brown." The man must have thought that I had lost my senses. But I was just about to acquire some sense.

I sued the theatre. I demanded not only my salary but also a relatively high indemnity. I sued the men who disrupted the meeting, and I sued the writer of the "flatfooted-peace-hyena" article.

All this would have as much result as the building of a tiny little wall against the Deluge. More, much more had to be done.

But was I not "non-political"? Did I not get into this political meeting somewhat by mistake? And does not he soil himself who touches dirt? Was it not enough if I washed off the dirt and rendered the dirt-mongers harmless by suing them?

It was by no means enough. I realized that my experience had nothing to do with politics—it was more than politics. It touched at the very foundations of my—of our—of the existence of all.

I had to bring this new viewpoint to the knowledge of my friends. They had to know what was brewing and that our whole, our passionate fervor was needed to repulse the attack. Then and there, we must unite on a defense program which should be constructive and militant and not just nice, conventional, and half-comprehensible.

But they were so dissimilar, my friends. Would it ever be possible to bring them together under one banner? And could the skeptical individualism of some, the careless liberalism of others, the social rebelliousness of still others, the gullible pacifism of yet another group—could all these be welded together in one strong unity?

I started my preparations. The small meeting was to take place in Berlin. There were not many whom I wished to invite. But they came from different classes and political ideologies. What I had in mind was a sifting and clarification of viewpoints and the finding of one common denominator.

3. A Political Meeting

The room in which the following scene took place was small, and consequently seemed crowded although not more than seven people were gathered there.

Scene—My room at the Hotel am Zoo, in Berlin.

Cast:

Hermann—Social-Democrat and trades-union man; intelligent, good-natured face; pedantically clean, a little threadbare, typically bourgeois clothes; quiet, reasonable manners.

Petrus—publicist and writer; long hair, horn-rimmed glasses, a tic-like twitching of the right eye; belongs to no party.

Heini—very young, some twenty years old, sportsman type, good-looking, carefree, non-political.

Georg—member of the Communist Party; blond, slim, quick; surprisingly assured in his demeanor; a trained speaker and keen debater. Middle thirties.

Alvin—convinced pacifist, Christian-humanitarian in tendency; gentle, and brunette; in his late twenties.

Siegfried—good-looking, elegant, obviously rich young man;

son of a banker. Pleasant, cultured personality. Twenty-five years old.

Myself—twenty-four years old, a young actress who has found out that it was not enough to mind one's own business.

That was the meeting. Of those present, *Hermann,* the Social-Democrat, *Siegfried,* the son of the banker, *Petrus,* the writer, and *Alvin,* the pacifist, were my personal friends. *Heini,* the very young and carefree one, was invited by Siegfried and had brought along *Georg,* the communist, whom he seemed to admire in a patronizing manner, which seemed strange, considering his age.

The room was full of smoke, even before we started to speak. There was nothing to drink, I wanted us to keep clear heads. I had bought a few small cookies which I served nicely arranged on soap containers and ash trays.

I was excited—and also hopeful. I examined the faces of my friends and found that they all looked kind and reasonable. I saw again the face of the Nazi with its hate-distorted mouth and shallow forehead onto which greasy hair fell. I thought: even if only in a small way, we're basically better than he. We have the better, the more human faces.

In my little opening speech, I reported to them my experience at the peace meeting. I had known very well, so I assured them, that somewhere in the country things like that happened every day. But now they had happened to me. And that, strange as it may seem, was "something else." I spoke of my doubts, about our weary, unconcentrated defensive attitude, and of my fear that the enemy might become stronger and more dangerous; and most of all that he might be closer than we thought. I also spoke of my own dislike of "politics" and of the fact that I had much rather act and read good books than "meddle."

"But now, we must 'meddle,' " I said, and looked challengingly around. "Because it is no longer 'politics' that is being played here. That which is coming upon us, if we let it come upon us, is the end. The end of all of us . . ."

I stopped, because I felt the eyes of my friends resting upon me with a slightly amused disapproval. "I don't mean to say," I finally said, and my voice sounded unsure, "that we all will be killed without much ado should 'that' come into power. But I do mean that we shall no longer have the right chance to live. Do you believe they will let us go on if they come into power? Do you believe your trade unions will continue to exist, your rights accepted? Do you believe we will be able to print what we like or live as we please? I, for my part, do not believe it. As we are sitting here, we might just as well pack up. Even the air we breathe will be exhausted as far as we are concerned. For that which is coming up here is vicious barbarism. It hates decency and reason with a passion of which we are not even capable—neither for the so-called 'good,' nor against the so-called 'evil.' But we must—"

Again I was confused. My friends, I knew, were more experienced in politics than I. They certainly saw things more realistically and felt that I was spinning tales and exaggerating in a childish manner. By no means must I ruin everything from the beginning of our meeting by suggesting panic. I controlled myself and said calmly and with conviction that the small circle which had gathered there was representative of nothing; it did not possess any power, no direct political influence. "But, if only we too would know exactly what we wanted, if only we could be united, and from tomorrow on, from tonight on, act together, then that *would* be important; it might even be *decisive.* Each one of us has friends; he belongs to a group, to a party.

Each one of us has his own professional and social class; his colleagues, his acquaintances. All those we must awaken! With all those we must work together! Believe me," I cried, "we all must 'meddle,' here and now. Or else everything will go wrong."

A short pause followed after I finished. Then Siegfried, the banker's son, asked for the floor. He said, "A purely technical question before the discussion starts. As far as I can see, we have representatives here of different political convictions. As a matter of fact, of almost all important convictions. There is no Catholic here, but Alvin represents the Christian viewpoint, and I know he represents it well. There is only one thing that strikes me. Why haven't we invited a National Socialist?" He blushed. "Not that I would like to see one," he continued. "Who *would* like to see one of those 'vicious barbarians'?" His ironical glance swept over me. "But it seems to me that opposition belongs in every democratic meeting. One should at least listen to what they have to say."

I said, "That is a misunderstanding, Siegfried. We are here to hold a democratic war council, not a democratic election meeting. And no one has ever yet invited the enemy to a war council."

Siegfried shrugged his shoulders. "Isn't your choice of the enemy somewhat arbitrary?" he wanted to know. "Aren't there people present who wish to destroy the democratic order much more manifestly than your 'enemy'?"

He did not look at Georg, the communist, as he spoke. But it was clear nevertheless who was meant.

I took refuge in my role of hostess and asked that the discussion not be made uncomfortable from the beginning by personal attacks.

Now little Heini spoke up for his friend and protégé, Georg. "Children," he said, and grinned in a friendly manner, "you act as if you were the League of Nations and had God-knows-what to decide. Your pseudo-seriousness is amusing, but it's all right with me. Only *I* brought Georg along and he is much more amusing than all of you together. You'd be lucky, Siegfried, to stand for half as much as Georg and be able to tell stories half as excitedly as he does."

Hermann, the Social-Democrat, who apparently had prepared some sort of a statement and was about to deliver it, cleared his throat. He had a sheet of paper in his hands.

"Oh," I said, hopefully, "Hermann wants to continue with the business before this meeting. Go ahead."

Hermann read:

"In all domestic as well as foreign matters," he said, "the trade unions have always followed a policy of constructivity and peace. We have made great strides in Germany; the standard of living and the cultural level of the laborers have risen considerably. With good cause the Social-Democratic Party is leading and will remain leading. That we have opponents, despite our advances made in these difficult times, is not only natural, it is even necessary in the interest of our democracy. Besides, we know of much more dangerous enemies than the Nazis, for the Nazis will eventually destroy themselves through the irresponsible and unintelligent nonsense which they propagandize. In any case," he said and looked up from his script, "in any case, I am absolutely opposed to the curtailment of the right of free speech and action of the opposition. The discontented must have voice, because then they feel better. Don't create martyrs! Nor deadly enemies! Social democracy is liberal and pacifistic, but it is also patriotic. We can, at least, understand the patriotism of the Nazis. We want to bring around the better and more sensible elements among them and win them over for our own cause. And because of that alone, we do not really want to 'fight' them."

Most of those present nodded in agreement. Only Georg uttered a short, derisive laugh and exchanged an understanding glance with little Heini.

I thought that Hermann was a little too smug and too satisfied with the successes of his party. It seemed to me that he was wrong in thinking the Nazis would "destroy" themselves through "the nonsense they propagandize." Nonsense, I thought, is exactly what the people want to hear when their own unemployed, unhappy lives cease to have sense. But I said nothing of the kind. Instead, I turned questioningly to Georg who obviously disagreed also.

I said, "Well, so we have come right to the point and have put up for discussion the question of free speech." I looked at Georg. "I was often told," I continued, "that your party intends to achieve its goal in an evolutionary manner within the frame of the existing order. It therefore must be interested in defending the existing order. Don't you think that certain liberties of the past should be curtailed so that the liberty of the whole be maintained?"

Georg shook his head.

"No," he said, "I don't think so. And I only laughed because those 'sozis' believe that they will gradually be able to win the Nazis over to their side. If anyone can accomplish that, we're the ones, for in their own way, the Nazis are revolutionaries too, entirely misguided revolutionaries—of course—but revolutionaries just the same. But as far as the curtailment of liberty proposed here is concerned, I am absolutely against it. For, in the first place, under the bourgeois system, any curtailment of freedom will work against us, the Left, and not against the Right. Only the revolutionary state, only dictatorship of the proletariat, has the right to curtail freedom for the good of all. The spirit in which such a thing would happen here would be retrogressive, reactionary. The reactionaries would win the upper hand even more so than now and we could see what we'd be in for. In the second place," he continued, and smiled shrewdly, "we certainly don't want a revolution now. We want, as you rightly said, to get to our goal within the frame of the existing order. But, if the existing order, rotten as it is, should fall apart by itself, if it collapses without our taking a hand in it, we will certainly be glad of that and welcome it. The National Socialists steal our ideas and twist them hopelessly. They call themselves 'socialists' and attempt to misguide the class-conscious laborers. In that they will not succeed; not in that. The fact, however, that they undermine the 'existing order' is to be appreciated. There is no doubt that the future belongs to us and to International Socialism. Everything that helps to bring about this future earlier is fine with us. And if the Nazis wish to hammer at the gates through which only we will storm in the end, so much the better!"

I was somewhat taken aback. Georg's argument made an impression on me. But it seemed to me that one had to be stronger, less in danger, more firmly established than our democracy, to risk such an experiment. He expected a disintegration of our general system through the burrowing of the Nazis and thought that we all would be better able to plow the ground once it had been loosened than in its present hard and unyielding state. But the ground was not hard and unyielding. It broke through as soon as one stepped on it. It was a weird moorland upon which we stood. We must reinforce it, not undermine it, and primarily, we must not allow the enemy to do the burrowing.

Heini, who had listened to his friend Georg with admiration and amusement, chuckled with satisfaction.

"At any rate, one thing we must take credit for," he said, "we're not dull. Something is always happening. Something is going on incessantly. Don't you think," he exclaimed, turning to the group, "that it is most amusing, our Germany? Political tension, which in the final analysis does not, God knows, interest me in the slightest, has at least resulted in a stimulating variety of turbulent activities in all fields. Take, for instance, the peace meeting at which our most honored hostess became aroused. How boring, how unnecessary would such a peace meeting be! We have peace—we're living in the middle of peace. And it is undescribably dull to go on chewing that monotonous fact over and over again. But, Dieu merci, a few youngsters in brown shirts come tearing in and bring life into this drab peace meeting. We should be grateful to them—and I personally am very grateful. I am grateful to you too," he said gaily and made a little bow toward his friend Georg. "You communists, too, bring some color into the drabness. To be frank with you, I like you better than those fellows in brown shirts, because you put such a scare into the bourgeoisie. It is incredible how much they fear you, and yet, fundamentally, you are as mild as lambs—or are you?"

Heini's cynicism made a generally unpleasant impression although it was disarmingly sincere. It was best to pass over his remarks in silence and to catch up with the discussion where Georg had concluded it. Siegfried seemed to be willing to do so.

"You all know," he said, "how much sympathy I feel towards the working classes. My father has given great sums for public education and the 'turnvereine.' I, myself, am most interested in our progressive, social theatre; that is also known. From the National Socialists I am, for obvious reasons, pretty far removed. Nevertheless, I prefer that movement in many respects to that of the communists. The National Socialists don't want a world revolution, they don't even want a 'revolution' in Germany. They want to correct certain mistakes which undoubtedly have been made. In the field of national and social problems they ultimately intend no evil. The fact that they employ rather crude methods and are seeking for all possible scapegoats in order to arouse and convert the masses is not very pleasant. But as the saying goes, 'You don't eat things as hot as they are cooked.' With time, those young billy-goats will dull their horns."

Heini chuckled. "The 'young billy-goats'! Siegfried—you are wonderful! And 'all possible scapegoats'! It is too bad the Nazis are so terribly anti-Semitic. You'd better admit that you would actually like them if it were not for this one 'scapegoat' upon which those 'young billy-goats' center their ruthless attacks. Does your father finance the Nazis too—or only the proletarian 'turnvereine'? It might not be a bad joke if he gave money to *all* his enemies—out of pure goodness and wise foresight."

That was going too far. Siegfried's face turned red with anger and embarrassment. "It is impossible to talk with you," he said, "you have not one ounce of seriousness."

Heini was absolutely without seriousness. He was a rich youngster who had no worries and who considered politics a terrific nuisance. Spoiled, and smug, it gave him great pleasure to compromise his family by showing himself everywhere with Georg, a communist. Incidentally, his father considered his son's improper friendship with a Leftist a sort of insurance in case the "Reds" should ever come to power. So he closed both his eyes to it. As for his real opinion, it was an open secret that Heini's father sympathized with the Nazis whom he considered the best bulwark against communism.

Heini's father, just as Siegfried's father, the Jewish banker, went so far as actually to finance the Nazis. So Heini had nothing to reproach Siegfried for on this point.

I thought that our meeting was losing ground, and tried to bring the group back to the subject at hand.

"Up to now," I said, "we've heard the voices of the Left center —Hermann; for the Radical Left, Georg; and the liberal capitalist voice of our friend Siegfried. Moreover, there was the voice of Youth—Heini's, if we wish to recognize Heini as its representative."

"No, he isn't!" everyone exclaimed, but Georg said, "He is, to a certain degree. He is inquisitive, careless, skeptical and ignorant. Many, very many, young people are like that in this country."

Heini accepted that as a compliment. "You see?" he exclaimed, "I am absolutely representative."

I said, "Be that as it may. Till now, any readiness for action here has not been great. For various practical reasons, reasons of political tactics, our friends have refused to form a strong, united front of defense against the rising tide of barbarism. Alvin," and I turned to the religious pacifist, "what is your stand in this matter? According to your whole attitude, only ideals affect your decision. Don't you think that we should act in order to retain our peace and freedom?"

Alvin nodded in agreement but at the same time, he shrugged his shoulders in a strange manner. He said, "You are both right and wrong. Of course, it would be horrible if the National Socialists should gain power here."

"But they have power," I interrupted him, "they already have."

And I told them that my contract for the summer festival had been cancelled just because the Nazi Party threatened to boycott the theatre. Alvin smiled gently and wisely.

"That is very, very sad," he said. "But I do not think it is to be wished that such things be given great publicity. If we exaggerate and build up the danger and the ruthlessness of those foolish young people to the outside world, to our English and French friends, we only endanger our peace work and our co-operation with the well-meaning of all nations. Insofar as the defense fight *within* the country is concerned, may I say that phrase is utterly repulsive to me. We do not 'fight.' We do not want to fight ever again. What is much more necessary is to spread the knowledge that fighting and war have never, never brought betterment, that they are not a solution. 'Fighting' is not our cause. We want to enlighten; not to be 'victorious.' Of course, it would be better if the political parties of the center had not gone so far away from Christianity and its teachings. One can be a political realist without losing sight of morality. No doubt our democracy would be more convincing to the youth, if it offered them a more attractive morale. That should be the aim of our national and international peace associations. Of course, a long time will pass before our work will bear fruit, but in the end, those fruits will be mature and even you, the political realist, will eat of it."

I said, "But do we *have* so much time? Do you believe that they will leave us the time we seem to need? I don't know, but it seems to me we are all falsely assuming that the danger is not great, not very imminent, not very 'dangerous.' I wish I could agree with you. In fact, to a certain extent I did agree inwardly with each one of you as long as he spoke, but the sum of everything said offers no program. Why is that?"

It was noticeable that Petrus, the writer, had been absolutely quiet, absolutely passive, until now. His right eye twitched, and he continuously ran his slender, hypersensitive fingers through his long hair. From time to time, he looked at the ceiling as if in desperation and shook his head. But he said nothing. And I knew that he had a most pertinent way of expressing himself when he wanted. Now suddenly he rose from his seat.

"Yes, why is that?" he repeated. "I will tell you. We have no program because we have no convictions, and we have no convictions because we have been lied to and cheated since we were able to say 'Mama'! We have no convictions because everything that was placed before us was bad and rotten. Look at me," he cried out, and looked down at himself with sincere and at the same time a somewhat self-indulgent sadness, "Look at me. I am a typical product of our times. I look talented, don't I? And no doubt, I am talented. I have a tic in my right eye, but that doesn't mean much and is only natural. I got it in the Great War. My hair is long and my clothes shabby. That is natural too. I don't have the money to take care of myself because I don't get money for my talent. I write poems which are too good for the popular magazines and articles which are too sharp in their criticisms of the powers that be. The small periodicals in which they're published are hardly read. I am not willing to make the necessary concessions to any powers. Moreover, as I belong to no party, because all parties are bad and rotten, no one helps me and no one supports me. I am a 'pacifist,' naturally. I wouldn't like to acquire a tic in my left eye. But your peace as it is, isn't worthy of survival. I am a 'socialist,' naturally. I would like having a part of the money taken from the rich so that I might have a chance to have my hair cut. But a religion which sees its whole heaven in the socialization of production is not my religion. I don't care whether the ruling archangels are all-powerful by the right of nature and birth, or whether a 'state god' endows them with their power. Blessed are the simpletons," he cried, and ran his fingers again through his hair, "blessed are those who believe that everything will be for the best, and that our wonderfully liberal social-democracy will take care of everything. But blessed also are those childishly striving who believe that a democratic defense front against the rising barbarism will finally save us from destruction. No one can save us and nothing can save us. We are doomed." And his right eye twitched nervously.

Those present were silent and bewildered. Petrus with a short, sudden bow said, "I enjoyed hearing what you had to say. I will confess you have somehow moved me. But don't be afraid," he said, and spread his arms in a Christ-like gesture, "the great chaos will come. It must come. And it will be a salvation after this God-forsaken 'order' which is our lot now." He went to the door. "And thanks for the little cookies," he said, changing his expression. He turned around and left.

The meeting, so it seemed, was over. Despite different arguments, they all were agreed on one point: for the time being, nothing should be undertaken. It was unnecessary, inopportune, unpacifistic, unchristian, premature, or simply hopeless to undertake anything. It was against the "program" of the various parties to join together with the "program" of other parties. It was impossible to create a unifying program. We could have no "convictions" because we had been cheated too often. And was the "enemy" who had thrown such a scare and excitement into me really the enemy? Couldn't he be placated and won over?

But even should that be impossible: it takes two to fight and because we didn't want to fight, no fight could begin. If only we did not irritate the enemy, and didn't make a martyr out of him, then we would be secure. Not to speak of the fact that we were much stronger than the enemy. Besides, we had so many other worries. We must not endanger our democracy through an undemocratic curtailment of freedom. We must be on our guard for other enemies, the communists, for instance, against whom those Nazi-enemies were a welcome counterbalance. And finally, from the standpoint of communists, the enemy was only aiding in the undermining of a bad social order. Because the existing order was bad. Of that, not only the communists were convinced. Petrus, the writer, had pointed out in strong words how bad it was. Only that in its stead, he wanted chaos which he vaguely thought to be frightful, while the communists already had a new order in readiness.

And what did I myself want? Was I satisfied with the success of my little undertaking or was I disappointed? I did not know for sure. Partly the arguments of my friends appeased me, partly it seemed to me that they were short-sighted, egotistic, self-satisfied, and not very courageous. Even the passionately aggressive speech of my friend Petrus had not been free of smugness and egotism. And he wasn't basically very brave. And what about Alvin, the pacifist? And little Heini? Refusing to fight, I thought, does not mean that you escape fighting. It means nothing but leaving the choice of the moment of attack to the opponent who wants to fight. As far as Heini was concerned, to him the whole thing was a game, a joke and a spectacle. One had only to be on the watch and to look out that the joke wasn't carried too far. One shouldn't trust the tricks of the actors. One shouldn't let oneself be taken in.

On the whole, there was no reason to get excited. Even Siegfried, the banker's son, saw no immediate cause for alarm. It was extremely sad that the Nazis have chosen just this particular scapegoat—the Jewish scapegoat—and everything must be done to sidetrack that particular phase. But that would probably change by itself. Anti-Semitism was a demagogical trick which would be dropped as soon as it fulfilled its purpose. No, there really was no cause for alarm.

I opened the window which had been kept closed in order not to disturb our neighbors. In thick waves, the cigarette smoke floated out and formed little clouds in the mild air of the summer night.

They are probably right, my friends, I thought as I looked down on the bustling and well-ordered traffic on the Kurfürstendamm. "I've let myself be made nervous and frightened by those rowdies, the other day at the meeting. We mustn't lose our heads. We mustn't become hysterical and make an elephant out of a gnat. I should have done better to look around for a theatrical job for the summer and to mind my own business than to sit here at the Hotel am Zoo and act the politician. After all, our politics are in the hands of professionals who know their craft."

And I decided from now on, as far as I was concerned, not to do anything any more. For the time being, I wanted to sleep.

Before I took refuge in unconsciousness, I let the faces of my friends once more pass before me. It was strange: their familiar features appeared vague and blurred. They dissolved bewilderingly into one another. They were friendly faces; but one seemed just like the other, so formless were their outlines, so vague their expressions. Then another, a strange face came between my friends and me . . . I didn't know it, I refused to recognize it. Over a low forehead, fell greasy, crumpled blond hair. Mouth and eyes were wide open. The mouth yelled, even the eyes seemed to shout. But there was nothing vague, nothing formless in this face. Of course, there was nothing friendly in it, either. That face hated; it was stamped and distorted by hate. It burned with hate. But while it seemed to shout senselessly, it knew well how to weigh its words. Behind this stupid low forehead, thoughts sharpened by hate crouched dangerously. The horrible face was a living lie. The words of that face distorted the truth as hate distorted its features.

I did not want to see that face any more, nor hear its lying words. I let myself slip deeper into the darkness. But it followed me even there. It shouted; it burned; it grew. It filled the room with the horror of its inhuman hate. Where were the faces of my friends?

4. The Resistance Fails

The end came sooner than anyone thought. In August, 1930, we had still been betting as to whether the Nazis would have as many as fifty, or considerably less than fifty, representatives in the Reichstag after the elections. But in September, they walked into it with 107 representatives. The Communists also made gains. After this catastrophic defeat of the democratic center, the headline of the leading liberal papers in Berlin read: "Parties In Power Still Leading."

At any rate, everywhere people were a little uneasy and frightened. But did they unite? Did the church fight side by side with the middle parties? Did the moderate and radical left fight together? Did Capital come to the support of the defense battle?

Nothing of the sort happened. As before, each group, each party, pursued its special interests, its special business, and each group and party, moreover, hoped to use the enemy for its own special purposes. As before, each group and party thought: Maybe the enemy is wild and vicious. But, in the first place, he is not my personal enemy. He hates the Jews (for whom I do not care much myself); he hates the Communists (whom I hate too); he hates the western democracies (whom I do not like myself); he hates our government (against which I have much to say myself); I, myself—my class, my religious beliefs—were not actually endangered by the enemy. And, besides, the enemy is far away. An *ocean of time* lies between us.

Everyone thought so. And all their discussions and preparations had a theoretical, absolutely unreal quality. It was as if they winked at each other and said: Of course, it is right and purposeful for us to talk *now* about what will happen on a faraway day when the enemy shall turn against us. We are farsighted and, theoretically, we do not think that this is out of the question. But it is apparent even now that there will be time enough then for us to seek help. Collectively, we are stronger than the enemy.

They *were* stronger—they could have been stronger.

Short-sighted egotism, lack of imagination and insight into the psychology of the enemy, false love of peace, lack of moral feeling, lack of voluntary discipline, lack of responsibility for the whole, a crippling mixture of skepticism and vague gullibility and a lack of spirit—all these dug the grave of democratic Germany.

Not the strength of the enemy, not even the strength of his henchmen, his German financiers and international bosses helped the enemy to victory. The resistance had failed! The fortress was ready to fall!

On the 30th of January, 1933, Adolf Hitler was appointed Chancellor of the Reich. On February 28, the Reichstag in Berlin burned down and all the opponents of the Nazi regime (for it still had opponents) were accused of having set fire to it. On March 5, general elections were held which resulted in dictatorial powers for the Chancellor even in Bavaria, the stronghold against Nazism.

But even now, while anyone in Germany remained who had the slightest power, the slightest influence—above all, while a coalition of all powers, and sum of all influences might have become dangerous to him, the dictator carefully avoided starting a general attack. Carefully, strategically, absolutely familiar with the psychology of his enemy, he rid himself gradually of one after the other. He began, as is generally known, with the unpopular minorities. No one could resent it much if he got rid of the Jews and Communists. When he started his fight against the Church, he rightfully counted on the calm indifference of large parts of the nation, especially when he pretended that it was not religion which he wanted to destroy but only the corrupt, sexually pathological and politically stubborn and unpatriotic priests misled by Rome. The war against the freedom of spirit was also not dangerous. Outside the victims themselves, no one seemed to take this war seriously.

Everything went step by step. Group after group, class after class succumbed. In the meanwhile, the rest just sat and waited. They remained neutral. The security of anyone who exposed himself carelessly for "others" was endangered.

After they all were individually defeated: heavy industry,

agricultural, the city middle classes, church and science, art and education—when all the territories of the nation's existence were occupied by the enemy—it was definitely too late to put up a resistance.

With all its horrors, we were sure, this development had one good. The technique of the enemy became obvious. No one in the future could say any more that he was taken by surprise by it. Europe, the world, knew now what was in store for it. In the international sphere, that which happened in Germany would not be repeated elsewhere.

We left Germany on March 10, 1933. It was much that we gave up: Fatherland, language, home, position, fortune—and many of the friends whom we loved.

Here I ceased writing for a moment in order to recall the fate of those who, on that early summer day in 1931, had gathered in my Berlin hotel room for the purpose of planning a joint defense against the rising danger of barbarism. But they had come to the conclusion then that it was neither opportune nor desirable to do anything in our own "defense."

Hermann, the Social-Democrat, went into exile. His race-proud mind (which had not been far-sighted enough) and his honest heart (in which could not be aroused enough resentment at the needed moment) made it impossible to remain in Germany a spectator of German dishonor; besides, he would have been in great danger had he stayed there. And so he went into exile to lead the poor and haunted life of a reluctantly suffering refugee—first in Austria, then in Czechoslovakia, finally in Belgium and—in the end—in France. I used to see him occasionally during those years. Since France's fall I have, of course, not heard from him. Perhaps he has fallen into the hands of the

Nazis, or waits hopefully in some "unoccupied area" for a Mexican visa.

Petrus committed suicide. The "chaos" from which he expected salvation from an imperfect and evil order engulfed him. The "chaos" that came was so much lower, so much more miserable and mean than he had envisaged in his bitter resentment against the existing order; it was a bureaucratically and sadistically organized "chaos" which he, in his innocent radicalism, could not possibly imagine. He jumped out of the window of his furnished room on the night of June 30, 1934—after the carnage which the Fuehrer of the Germans had staged for his friends and intimates. Many hundreds of such friends and confidants had been murdered by the Fuehrer on that day. Petrus, the writer, the outsider, the skeptical anarchist with the twitch in his right eye, was by no means directly affected by that general purge. He was in no danger at the time; he could have enjoyed the fact that "salvation through chaos" was so obviously on its way. But he jumped out of the window. News of his death reached us long after his poor, limp body had found rest under the earth.

The friends . . . the friends of that time . . . the participants in that meeting. . . .

Heini, the twenty-year-old youngster and cynical connoisseur who had been grateful to the Nazis as well as to the Communists because they brought some life into "this drabness" —what has become of him?

As far as I know he is doing well. He became a flyer and was one of those heroes who, in September, 1939, turned helpless Warsaw into a shambles. Later on, thanks to the excellent connections which his wealthy father has always maintained with the Nazis, he was sent abroad. Once he turned up in the United

States. Somebody I know met him at a party. How had he managed to come over, he was asked—and how was it possible that he, a Nazi flyer—passed unhindered through the British-controlled Gibraltar? As an answer, he drew his passport proudly from his pocket—it was a German Jew-passport with a fat "J" on the first page. He, the hundred percent Aryan, had received it at home so that he might serve the Reich as an émigré. Later on, I heard that he went to South America in order to do his part in bringing some "life into the drabness." I can't believe that he is very happy in his position. His sense of humor can't be satisfied among the Nazis. Moreover, he was not really cruel by nature and probably will realize eventually how vile the life is to which he has sold himself.

Of his friend Georg, the communist, I've lost sight. For a long while, he was in the concentration camp at Oranienburg; we knew that this was one of the worst camps. He was beaten and badly mistreated. He survived and even was promoted to a higher position as a "group commander" in the camp. After two years of imprisonment, he was released as "converted." Since then, he has become a Nazi—only as a "pretext," as pure "deception," so his former comrades now in Belgium assured us. But inasmuch as shortly before the outbreak of war, he accepted a splendid and well-paid position in the Hermann Goering Works and, voluntarily or involuntarily, cut off every contact with all of us—I am not sure whether he is still only "pretending" or whether he really has been converted.

Alvin, the pacifist, the Christian, gentle opponent of our "defense attempts" is dead. He belonged to an international Bible group which displeased the Third Reich and was arrested in the midst of his efforts for peace and understanding among men. Although, or rather *because* he was one of the most harmless inmates of the camp into which he was thrown, the Storm Troopers, eager for action, chose him as the particular butt of their jokes and educational experiments of all sorts. We know that he had been forced to beat his co-prisoners and that in the end, he himself was beaten to death because he refused to kneel before Hitler's picture and to chant insulting verses against Christ. "As a matter of fact," a camp-mate of poor Alvin later reported, "he didn't really resist. By that time he was already far too weak to resist and far too weak to carry out the order. He simply collapsed and then they finished him. You must remember," our friend added, shaking his head wearily, "that nothing arouses and infuriates the Nazis so much as gentleness and helpless goodness."

Alvin is dead. He was very gentle, very helpless and very good.

Who else was there on that evening? Who else had in those days hoped that the enemy was no enemy at all, and that it was better not to undertake any unnecessary or even harmful steps? Siegfried—oh yes, Siegfried, the banker's son, who would not have disliked the Nazis had they chosen any other scapegoat for persecution than the Jewish one.

Siegfried escaped. He lives in Palestine from where he sometimes writes us melancholy letters full of self-accusation and remorse. His father, who had spent so much money on the one hand for the proletarian "turnvereine," and on the other, for the Nazi party, died of a heart attack—just at the right moment. And so the pogroms of November, 1938, could do him no more harm. Siegfried had written us of his passing away. "It was too much for him," he wrote us from Tel Aviv, "and his disappointment was too great."

They did not fare well, my friends who had met in my room

on that evening; it hurts to think of them and perhaps it would have been better if I had not digressed from my report and awakened this old pain.

How great was our sorrow—on that March 10, 1933—when we left our house?

It was quite evident, it was not small. Nevertheless we were basically hopeful. We were free and the nightmare, that horrible ghost which chased us away, would in turn be chased away by the will, the united activity of civilized Europe.

What happened then, what gradually was repeated step by step with appalling thoroughness, I don't need to describe. And anyway I am imposing upon my train companion, the young American, a reading of a story of suffering which, for the present, he is convinced has nothing to do with him. And he too knows, as well as I, that the resistance in Europe did not function. But what I must get over to him, nevertheless, is that the failure of resistance in Europe had the same causes as in Germany. Nothing was learned from our mistakes.

Ghastly! It was ghastly!

The talks which we had in those years between 1933 and 1939 with our friends in France and England, with the young Swiss, Dutchmen, Czechs, were all identical with our old discussions in Germany. Only now we were not so undecided, so unsure, soft and subject to influences. We at least knew what was happening. But we no longer had the power to put our knowledge to use. We were a scattered, homeless little group whose entreaties and warnings, whose every activity were met with suspicion as being inspired by resentment, as being maliciously or wantonly exaggerated, not objective, and not to be taken very seriously.

At any rate, so much was sure and so much we had to realize

to our greatest terror: For the time being, nothing, not the least thing, was to be undertaken in the defense of civilization. It was "unnecessary, inopportune, unpacifistic, unchristian, premature, technically wrong, or simply hopeless" to undertake anything. It was against the "program" of the individual countries to join in with the "programs" of other countries. Europe was unable to feel any convictions. It had been cheated too much. And was the "enemy" really an enemy? Couldn't he be appeased, and won over and used to advantage? But even if that should prove impossible—it takes two to fight. Inasmuch as "we" refused to fight, there would be no fight. If he was only not irritated, the enemy, one was secure. All the more secure as nothing was left undone in the way of "technical" security, exactly as in Republican Germany. Moreover, the "enemy" was by no means aiming at France or England. Also, Holland, Switzerland, Czechoslovakia or Poland had nothing to fear. All he wanted was to stamp out communism and that was good. And if, one faraway day, he really should want more and different things—well, there was still time to get together and collectively the democracies would be much stronger than he. But to start anything unitedly against him now was superfluous. France had different interests from England—Poland had no interest whatsoever in Czechoslovakia.

"Our order is bad and rotten," the young intellectuals in the western democracies cried. "It does not pay to defend it."

"Criminal interest groups want a preventive war against Germany," the pacifists of all countries cried in international meetings. "We are about to be cheated for the second time."

"It is still very interesting and stimulating in Berlin," the young traveling foreigners cried after returning from their study or pleasure trips. And in order to give themselves a more serious air, they added, "One must only understand the Germans. Then we can live in peace with them."

"It is sad, very sad," the most humanitarian among our acquaintances in Zurich, London and Paris said mildly and wisely when we spoke of the horrible deeds which were being committed all the time in our lost country. "But it might be well to see the good, the hopeful and not only the evil. If we want to cooperate with Germany—and we must want it for the sake of peace—we must not exaggerate the danger and the ruthlessness of the young German government."

Our reason and our hearts were aroused when we heard such talk. It was an outrage of the reasoning power when thinking people denied what was proved and the eye declared the obvious, invisible.

Had nobody read *Mein Kampf*? Did nobody read the *Völkischer Beobachter*? Was the extent of the German rearmament unknown? Wasn't the German talent for organization, German shrewdness in the service of the new German government, a threat beyond belief? Was it not seen what was going on within Germany and was it not known that all those things were dress rehearsals for a world-wide "première"? They believed the peace talks and promises of the Fuehrer. Had he not delivered these same speeches in Germany, given the same promises? And had not each one been cheated, one after the other? Was it conceivable, was it imaginable that the old anti-communist trick could work even in the international sphere? Europe was convinced that Nazi Germany would turn only against Russia and Jewry. Why was it convinced? Because Hitler said it would be so. But he had said the same in Germany.

It was a heartfelt blow to experience this calm indifference, this moral impotence with which the German misdeeds were accepted everywhere in Europe. The failure of resistance up to September 3, 1939—the collapse of the European Neutrals after September 3, 1939—the Belgian treason—the French collapse—they all were consequences of that moral impotence, of that lack of real and spontaneous rage in the presence of wrong and barbarism.

Vainly did we plead that our fight against the Nazis, and our appeal for the sympathy of the world was not, or at least not primarily, motivated by the plight of our friends in the German concentration camps. And that not for ourselves did we wish sympathy. We deserved our plight, we thought, because we had failed. Our country was lost and destroyed because we did not see the danger in time and we did not fight passionately enough. "It is no longer just Germany that is at stake," we cried out. "It is you—it is your countries—your democracies—your freedom—your lives."

We already knew that the cause of morality, propriety, truth, justice, would not impel anyone to raise a finger where "tactics," willingness to concede, and ostrich politics were all-powerful. It was senseless to expect our foreign friends to "fight for an ideal." But, we used to say, the Nazis have killed everything in Germany that makes life worth living and that makes man's living together possible. And whoever sees the murder with open eyes and lets it happen without interfering makes himself an accessory to the crime. "German rearmament," we pointed out, and said, "Hitler wants to rule the world—your world!"

With slightly amused disapproval, the glances of our friends rested on us.

"Children, children," our friends said, "you are of course furious to the core and you see everything black. But it is neither so dark, nor so simple as you see it. We must let things develop and give those young billy-goats over there a chance to dull their horns."

An ocean of space and time seemed to lie between our friends and the danger. We fought, we argued. But our voices faded into nothingness. We were poor, ghost-ridden fools. Foolish, pathetic, hysterical in our misfortune. One shouldn't let oneself be unnerved by us. One shouldn't believe everything that we said and especially one shouldn't let oneself be pushed by us into unpremeditated acts. One should wait, watch, gain time. And in doing so, they waited just the time which the enemy needed in order to prepare himself quietly. And step by step they lost position after position.

The victorious western democracies allowed the enemy to change their victory of the World War into defeat. So exactly did the German victors of 1918, the German Democrats and Republicans yield to the enemy. In actuality, strategically, the democratic western powers between 1933 and 1939 lost one fortress after the other, one spearhead after the other. Even worse, because they also began sliding down in the sphere of morality, they lost also one moral position after the other. They lost prestige in the outside world and self-assurance, power and moral backbone within.

The young French intellectuals were no longer saying only "Our order is bad and rotten." They rather said, "Our order is miserable; it is not one iota better than the order in Nazi Germany which you want us to fight."

But that was their fatal mistake. Already they had lost much through their own fault. Oh, they did not even dream how much more there was to be lost!

"We have given up Abyssinia," they exclaimed dejectedly.

"We have betrayed Spain," the progressive young Englishmen wailed. "We have sold out Austria!"

And the young Frenchmen closed the sad concert with their, "We have sacrificed Czechoslovakia, our ally, our wall in the East."

But we ask ourselves whether the pained anger of our friends was absolutely sincere, whether it was entirely justified. It came a little post-mortem—that was sure. For, had public opinion during the English betrayal of Abyssinia, Spain, Austria, and Czechoslovakia taken a clear and united stand against such betrayal, it would never have taken place. No democratic government, no parliament, no Tory clique, no congress, no senate, is able to impose upon a people anything which it really and clearly does not want. Only a dictatorship is in a position to do that.

But dictatorship comes as infallibly as the "amen" after a prayer, as soon as a nation, made bewildered and unhappy by difficulties and crises from which it sees no way out, morally weakened through too many mistakes and crimes of omission, through concessions to the evil and too many betrayals of the good, betrayals to which it has itself given its consent—when such a nation has lost confidence in itself. Dictatorship comes as soon as a nation has no more power to remain unified and faithful. Dictatorship comes as soon as a nation no longer sees the moral abyss that lies between dictatorship and democracy. But a nation cannot perceive this abyss if democracy itself has covered it over with weakness, dissension, and lack of faith, with self-betrayal, and betrayal of its ideals, with rotten willingness to concede, and with a plaintive liberalism which, pretending to be the real and most important symbol of democracy, throws the gates wide open to the enemy. Dictatorship comes when a nation, without knowing it, is ripe for it. Dictatorship comes when the "resistance" fails.

It will happen either—as in the case of Germany—that an enemy from within will undermine democracy and erect its dictatorship, or—as in the case of France—the enemy inside will surrender the fortress to the aggressor on the outside.

Other forms of a democratic collapse are also imaginable. The enemy within and without might weaken and disorganize the democracy of a country to such an extent that it would be entirely unable to put up a resistance. Inasmuch as it would not fight, it would be unnecessary in such a case to formally surrender it to the enemy on the outside. The democracy would rather slip, step by step, over to the enemy on the outside. He would have nothing to do but, in close collaboration with the enemy within, interpenetrate it completely and occupy its key positions, without the necessity of making his victory too obvious.

That would be possible too.

We don't like to think of it. We don't want to think of it.

But one thing we know. The greatest effort of which a nation is capable, the passionate cooperation of all, the most stubborn self-confidence and an unlimited confidence in the integrity and wisdom of the government chosen by the people—all this and more is necessary to make the "resistance" function. But what is most and above all necessary, is a recognition of the closeness and greatness of the danger.

I had spent the whole day writing. I didn't even go into the dining car. Partly because I wanted to save time, partly because I didn't want to see the young American for whom this scribbling was intended. He might have smiled at me skeptically and robbed me of my courage to put down on paper the things which I wanted to point out.

But I must tell him tomorrow that he must not believe that I was superficial or unthoughtful, because I wrote down so much in so short a time. I was trying to give a résumé of the thoughts which have not left my mind for one single minute for seven years. It does not take much time to write down things that you have thought over and over again.

Had I made them clear—my long familiar thoughts?

A picture rises within me which again is not a new one. Nevertheless, it seems to me that it has lost nothing of its sharp urgency. It is a simple comparison but it holds true whichever way you look at it. When neighboring houses are on fire, there is only one thing to do: help put it out before it spreads over to our own house. It is senseless to wait until next week when a new, a better extinguisher will be delivered. It is senseless to refuse to waste our water on a fire in someone else's house, even if this other one should not be without blame for this fire. Because once the fire has spread to our own house, it may become so big, so overwhelming that our water reserve may not suffice to quench it. It is also possible that, poisoned and blinded by the smoke all around, we might not be able to put our water reserve to its best use. It is particularly senseless to argue with one's roommates about the possibility perhaps of not extinguishing the fire now but somehow hindering its spreading to one's own house by throwing it a few mattresses in order to appease its hunger and so content it. That all this is senseless is obvious.

And I can already see the mocking expression of my young American friend and hear his "That's obvious, but nobody would be quite so silly." Nobody? I wonder. . . .

3

CONVERSATION IN THE SUN

As agreed upon, I handed the "report" to my American friend before leaving the train.

"So you actually did it?" he said thoughtfully, weighing the pile of papers crowded with my minutely written words in both his hands.

I said, "Of course it is most incomplete. I mean, it is only a sketch, a sketched but sincere self-portrait. Nevertheless, I am pretty certain that you will recognize the resemblance—the appalling resemblance between what *we* were then and what *you* are today."

We were both standing surrounded by a ring of luggage in the splendid new terminal at Los Angeles.

With a proud motion of his hand the young man pointed out the magnificent, well-designed, beautiful building.

"Butter instead of cannons," he said, "and handsome new terminals instead of barracks."

I nodded, and we shook hands over the piles of suitcases.

He said, "It was a pleasure to have met you. But we shall have to discuss this."

And again he acted as if the weight of my manuscript were pressing him down.

"Certainly," I agreed. We decided to drive out to the ocean one day soon in order to settle the "whole thing" definitely.

Then we parted.

I was looking forward to this new meeting with as much excitement, anxiety, uncertainty, expectancy and impatience as if very much, as if everything depended upon it—my own future and the future of the world.

If he calls me up today to make the appointment, I thought childishly, then everything will be all right. Tomorrow—that will be pretty bad; but the day after tomorrow—that will be disastrous.

He called "today." That was splendid.

The ocean was blue, the sky radiant and the flowers, bushes and palms were bathed in an unearthly light. But we gave only an occasional glance to the magnificence around us. No sooner were we settled in the car, shortly after my American friend called for me, than we turned our attention to the subject which was the reason for this meeting.

"I've studied your paper thoroughly," the young man said. "I found many things in it which are true and horrifying, but also some that appear incorrect. Or rather, a little inexact and falsely emphasized."

My head drooped like that of a pupil who is handed back unsatisfactory homework.

"In my opinion," he continued, "you have approached the problem from a purely psychological and ethical angle, without giving sufficient consideration to the actual political and economic conditions. And so, while in the ethical and psychological spheres there might be some dangerous resemblance between us here and Republican Germany on the one hand, and democratic Europe on the other hand, in the essentially political and economic spheres, our situation is entirely different. Am I right?"

We were driving along the palm-shaded highway from Santa Monica to Santa Barbara. As my young friend was driving and had to keep his eyes on the road with its heavy traffic, we did not look at each other during this conversation. We both stared straight ahead and talked as if delivering a kind of soliloquy.

I reflected. "Are you right? Not entirely. You believe in the doctrines of Karl Marx, I presume?"

He seemed slightly embarrassed. "If I believe in Marx?" he smiled—"what a delicate question! . . . He was a pretty great fellow, I suppose, and his ideas may help us to grasp a lot of things that otherwise would seem rather muddled. Think of Fascism, for example—or Nazism. . . ."

"I always keep thinking of them," I interrupted him, with a little laugh that hardly sounded very gay. "Although there are so many other matters to think of—and more pleasant ones, too. . . . However, we are bound to brood on Fascism—even when the sun is shining as now, and the sea is so tremendously blue. . . . We are doomed to discuss Fascism. Now, does Marx really make you *understand* that bloody mystery?"

"I think he does," he said firmly, and added, with a somewhat apologetic smile, "at least up to a certain degree. . . ."

"Up to a certain degree!" I repeated swiftly. "There you are! I agree with you that Marx tells nothing but the truth. But it is not the *whole* truth he says. He has discovered certain new aspects of truth—very significant aspects, to be sure, but the complete truth, as you yourself rightly said in our conversation on the train—the complete truth is more complex, more involved, more horrible, more inspiring. . . . It's all right to say that Fascism is just a last, desperate effort of Capitalism to defend itself against the inevitable rise of Socialism; that it's nothing but another manifestation, another virulent crisis of the everlasting class struggle that determines the course of all human history. That is an easy and convincing interpretation of what happened in Europe. I don't say it's erroneous. But I insist that it is only a part, a certain aspect of truth and not even a decisive one. You say: Nazism was prepared and established as a militant defense mechanism against Communism. All right. But how, then, did it work? It worked as a sort of perverted revolution, the 'Revolution of Nihilism,' as Rauschning has named it. It did not defend Capitalism but destroyed civilization. It surpassed all limits of a class struggle which, after all, was conceived, originally, as a process *within* the sphere of civilization. But Fascism is the rebellion of barbarism: the jungle against the order. . . . How do you explain, then, so puzzling and alarming a phenomenon? Neither political nor economic explanations are quite sufficient. There are more mysterious forces involved: age-old impulses, eternal human desires; the diabolic lust of destruction, the infantile rebellion against law and order; the Evil *as such,* if you know what I mean. . . . This may sound rather mystic. But I mean it in a sober way. I must try to tell you that, to explain the ghastly phenomenon that is Hitler, the Marxian doctrine is not sufficient. Rather may the doctrines of analytical psychology help us in clarifying those appalling events. I am afraid, though, that even such lucidity as they have achieved is not penetrating enough to throw light into that lurid darkness. We need something else to overcome that paralyzing fear and apprehension which is the result of our *not-understanding*. We need Faith, which is the most mysterious and at the same time simplest of all notions. . . ." He nodded pensively. "Faith, it sounds fine, very fine, indeed. We must have faith, of course! . . . But don't you think that, on the other hand, those big words and sublime notions are a trifle dangerous, too? They could divert us from the more realistic aspects of things. 'Diabolic Rebellion,' 'Revolution of Nihilism'—O.K. And still I believe the paramount reason for Mr. Hitler's success was Germany's poverty which caused the deadly crisis of German Capitalism!"

"Right," I said, "or, rather, right, again, to a certain degree. For though it may be true that Nazism wouldn't have come into being were it not for Germany's status as a 'have-not-nation,' it is just as true that the actual Nazi successes are not *based* on existing economic conditions, that they were achieved in spite of those conditions and for reasons that lie entirely in the psychological and ethical field. Nobody could be poorer than Germany was, poorer in gold and poorer in raw material. Also nobody could appear to have less political power or influence than Germany in 1933. This may have caused the rebellion on her part. But what did cause its success? Hitler was successful, because, in the psychological and ethical sphere the surrounding world failed in its defense fight. Economically and politically this world was in a far, far better condition than Nazi Germany. Nevertheless it drifted irresistibly toward the moment when it had to fight for its bare life, and even that is now almost lost. Why? For what reasons? Because of mistakes which couldn't be remedied any more; because of an irretrievable loss of time which had its source in ethical and psychological attitudes, and not in economic and 'essentially political' conditions. Am *I* right?"

A bay opened up before us. My American friend parked the car on a grass-covered spot from which we had a most beautiful view of the water and the magnificently curved highway lined with palm trees.

"Maybe," he finally answered. "But what do you want us to do? Don't you think that a country at war or in a state of preparation for war necessarily disintegrates ethically to such an extent that in the end it forgets what it is fighting for? Don't you think it is better for us to keep ethically intact, to keep our democracy intact, and thus, after the rest of the world has fallen to pieces, still to remain a last haven of freedom, decency, and peace?"

We had left the car and were seated, side by side, on the grass.

"My God!" I exclaimed, "how convincing that sounds, and how mortally wrong it is! Haven't you found out yet that one cannot keep 'morally intact' by giving free course to the infernal disaster? Don't you see yet that this firebrand, this plague will stop nowhere, and that it is up to us to put an end to it if we don't want to be corroded, be devoured by it? Has France's example, the example of England, and that of the European Neutrals made no impressions on you whatsoever? Don't you realize that the world has shrunk through the achievements of man's genius and that right now, this minute, the world has to decide in which direction it wishes to rotate in the future, whether to the light of progress and reason—or to the shadows of a most inhuman barbarism? An 'in between' no longer exists. Things have gone too far already. And it is America, it is your country, it is you who will have to make the decision. I beg you for the sake of all that you love, that you value—make the right decision."

The young man laughed. "I?" he exclaimed. "I am a student, a nobody, a grain of sand on the beach. Why do you pick on me?"

I shook my head in desperation. "You are a typical and—I beg your pardon—a very good representative of the youth of this country," I said. "If you refuse to recognize the truth and to live by it in your emotions and actions—then things are really in a very bad way."

He became serious at once. "Well," he said, "I can only repeat, What do you want us, what do you want me, to do?"

"In those seven years," I said, "the European democracies might have had a chance to save themselves and to avoid the catastrophe of this war, if they had kept themselves 'ethically intact' and had fearlessly done the right thing. America, the most powerful democracy in the world, still has that chance. As things are today, it *looks* as if democracy, due to its structure and principles, were incapable of keeping discipline in times of peace; that war must come before democracy decides on strong, swift, determined and united action. As things stand today, it *looks* as if democracy simply were inferior to the totalitarian system, and as if it were doomed to take action only when it is already too late. But that is not true! Democracy is not inferior and is not doomed! What a fatal defeatism lies in the belief that Hitler is irresistible and that his mastery over Europe, yes, over the world, was our historical fate. On the other hand, what a terrible mistake it is to assume that he will stop all by himself and that our will for peace alone is enough to stop him. That is not enough. Neither are battleships completed in 1944. 'Men Must Act' is the title of a book by a clever and brave American. We must act, now—not 'later,' not too late. Why do your politicians, despite their undeniable love of America, fight each other to the last at a moment when from the outside the knife is already pointed at the throat of your country? Why do your industrialists make only 896 planes a month when admittedly they are capable of producing thirty times as many? Why do they do that at a moment when a few thousand airplanes might decide this war for America without the necessity for you and those like you to die and, probably, to die in vain? Why do you oppose universal conscription and why will you come to accept it only when it is too late? Why don't you want to see the truth? Why don't you see that you're doing exactly what Hitler wants you to do—namely, almost nothing?"

My young friend, his eyes again tinted with the grey-black color which I had already noticed on the train, exclaimed: "I beg your pardon. Nothing? Almost nothing? Our preparations are enormous. We will have to pay taxes until we'll all be impoverished. We're getting ourselves into wonderful shape—slowly but surely. And as far as our politicians are concerned—that is a consequence of democracy and all that which we wish to maintain."

"I'm sorry," I said. "I was too vehement. Please forgive me. But there are thoughts and actions which, although objectively good and right, one cannot afford in certain situations. Thoughts and actions which are erroneous and suicidal when contemplated at the wrong and critical moments. I will give you an example. The young English intellectuals—even many of the Communists among them—were men of great good will. In 1938 they still talked of immediate social reforms as the first problem. They were drawing blueprints for an ideal house to be built in the future—and meanwhile somebody else was getting ready to bomb the very foundations on which this future could be built. They too thought it was just a matter of taxes and reform. But if you let democracy go, its reforms go with it—not only the ones it has now, but the ones a good future might bring."

After a short silence, the young man said, "You are not an American yet, you are, so to speak, a stranger here. Don't you think that you are amazingly frank? What I mean is, aren't you afraid that you might go too far and that it might be better for you not to mingle in our affairs too much?"

He said that in the friendliest fashion and as if more worried than resentful. I answered immediately without thinking about it.

"I am not afraid of that," I said. "That is, I am not concerned with what might be 'better for me.' Everything is at stake now—the very lives of all of us are at stake. If we let Hitler win, then he will rule the world. But it will be a ruined, a horribly desolate world which he will rule and our lives would be meaningless. Neither you nor I could breathe in such a world. Already he has ruined the Continent, already he is threatening to ruin the British Empire. Wherever he steps there is no longer life: the flourishing agriculture of Holland and Denmark—they are wrecked and devastated. France's civilization—shattered and in ruins. I don't need to enumerate all the countries and cultures which have bled and died. They all hoped to save themselves by being concerned with their own, only their own security. They all have allowed the murderer to assassinate the neighbor, one after the other until their own turn came, and they were helpless, isolated, corroded by the poison which they had let penetrate their own bodies. And now America? What are you concerned with? Security for yourselves? There is no such thing. There is only a world which offers security to all—or one which means destruction, retrogression and barbarism for all. Let Hitler be victorious in Europe—and work behind your Maginot Ocean and stretching out before you the ocean of time in which you believe and which does not exist! Rearm for the year 1944. Fight tooth and nail among yourselves in internal political quarrels. Let your people believe the danger is far away and that one can, without fear of punishment, be both a hundred percent neutral and, at the same time, vitally interested in the victory of one party. Or let your people believe that America will be able somehow to come to terms with Hitler's Europe.

Let them believe that this time, in the exceptional case of America, the 'appeasement' will work out and that it can be ethically defended. Persuade them that the 'exceptional country' America will be able to continue existing as a free and rich democracy when the rest of the world is in ruins and on those ruins crouches the anti-Christ while his apostles growing in numbers within your country are preparing for an attack against you. . . . Am I going too far? Am I a stranger? Am I meddling in other people's affairs? There is only one affair—the affair of mankind—and that is my affair as well as yours. Into the hands of America, into your hands, God has placed the affairs of mankind. And one man should be forbidden to entreat you: 'Act! This is your hour, it's the final hour—the Zero Hour!' "

Exhausted, I stopped. My friend was listening in silence. Now, having finished, I was a little ashamed of my emotionalism. I had let myself go, I thought, and it is probably not clever to be so terribly frank. But then again, I thought: Only the truth, the pure and full truth should be spoken from now on. And what I have said was the truth. To the devil with "tactics," with pseudo-clever and insincere strategy, to the devil with diplomacy in a world where murderers disguised as diplomatic representatives of the mortal enemy walk around freely in peace, and in their "immunity" prepare for the last monstrous crime. To the devil with egotistic and cowardly "caution" in a world which has been ruined by egotistic and cowardly caution.

The young man gave me a long and searching look. When he finally answered, there was warmth and friendship in his tone. What he said had weight although it was clothed in light words.

"O.K.," he said. "I see."

III

THEY SAY IN THE COLLEGES . . .

McGEORGE BUNDY

III

THEY SAY IN THE COLLEGES . . .

THE NATION faces a crisis—we know it faces a crisis—of course we do. Take it in the field of its clearest manifestation, the tools of war. A year ago it was only the big-navy men who called for "a navy second to none"; today the country almost unanimously supports a program which is to give us a navy larger by far than any other in the world. A year ago our army was a joke; we knew it and did not care. Today the army is sorely tried to spend the billions given it by an anxious Congress, and peace-time conscription, an unheard-of policy for Americans, is supported by two-thirds of our people. These are the blunt facts. Behind them is the crisis itself.

It is not hard to see that every part of our lives is going to be affected. Already we can feel the changes coming. Friends of mine who never worked in their lives are training for the army and navy reserves. Girls who by their own admission were not made for physical exertion are scrubbing floors and shaking thermometers as they painfully acquire the elements of nursing. My family, which had not for years seen anything in short pants or pigtails, has made room for a couple of very small subjects of King George. And even if reserve training camps are not bad fun, if the hospital corridor is as good a place as any for gossip, if two little children are a small expense and a large pleasure, these changes still are signs of a serious time. In the beginning, any great national movement seems a little like a game—but this game involves us all. It is going to be long, and the stakes are high. It is not a joke that our thoughts have come to include war as a possibility not so very remote. It is not a joke that our nerves will no longer let us listen to the radio. There is nothing funny, any more, about Adolf Hitler.

For college men, the facts are as pressing as for any other group in the country. They will be conscripted; if any of us fight, they will. To any undergraduate, therefore, the national crisis has an acute personal meaning. Even those of us who have bad eyes and worse feet do not look for any escape from the iron hand of national necessity.

But it is not the facts themselves that worry us. We are young enough to adjust ourselves to almost any material change. The real problem is not *how* we shall do these things, but *why*. I am not therefore going to discuss ways and means of satisfactory adjustment to the changes forced by our new national attitude. Such things will take care of themselves. My concern is rather with the purposes and ideals with which the changes are to be met. In the struggle to maintain freedom—and it is exactly that—there is no hope for us if we do not clearly understand what we are defending and to what end we defend it.

Obviously I cannot put myself forward in such a difficult discussion as a spokesman of "the undergraduate viewpoint." There is no homogeneity of undergraduate thought on the subject, and I personally have generally found myself, in any particular discussion, in the minority. Few persons are more irritating than those who go about saying *Youth* thinks this, or *Youth* is opposed to that. It is true that there are important respects in which the thinking of the younger generation is in general different from that of its parents. But the concept of Youth, as a special-interest group, is one of the less satisfactory by-products of modern thought. The thinking of the undergraduate is important, and its nature should be carefully studied by people of all ages. But if we who are young set ourselves up as a pressure group, believing that because of our age we have a special set of ideals and purposes, we are only self-important and foolish. This is the unfortunate error of youth groups and undergraduate petition-writers the country over. The differences between youth and age do not constitute grounds for a class struggle.

My object, then, is to discuss the various peculiarities of undergraduate thinking, the things that have made us think as we do, and the mistakes which I think we must speedily rectify if we are rightly to understand and meet the shape of things to come. I speak not for my fellows but about them.

The proper starting point for any individual in a discussion of this kind is a statement of his own convictions. There is no one, I hope, who looks with a wholly dispassionate eye at the controversy over foreign policy. Anyone who claims to have no opinion is a fraud or a fool, and anyone who tries to write without stating his beliefs is like a navy without a base—confused, ineffective, and vulnerable.

Any given opinion about foreign policy is not materially affected by the age or sex of the person holding it. When I have said, therefore, that I am in hearty agreement with the views that have been expressed in earlier chapters, it will not be necessary for me to recapitulate in detail the things that make me believe as I do. Let me then put my whole position in a sentence. I believe in the dignity of the individual, in government by law, in respect for the truth, and in a good God; these beliefs are worth my life, and more; they are not shared by Adolf Hitler, and he will not permit them to me unless he has to; I therefore believe that my efforts, and those of the countrymen with whom I share my beliefs, must be energetically given to their defense; I do not think Hitler a weak or negligible antagonist, and I believe that if we are to have our way and not his, we must act swiftly and vigorously; such a course involves sacrifice and evil, but to a smaller degree than the alternative of surrender. It was a long sentence, and even now the picture is incomplete, but perhaps the reader will be able to fill it in as I proceed to consider the attitudes that are characteristic of my college contemporaries, the mistakes I think they make, and the things that all of us must do. I earnestly hope that I shall not appear to be lecturing out of any self-admitted and boundless wisdom. I have things to say that I think are important; the reader will remember, even if I forget, that they came from a college graduate, vintage 1940. The source of all my evidence is my experience and my reading in nine years at Groton and Yale.

The position which has been taken from various starting points by each of the writers of this book is not popular in the colleges. For one reason or another most undergraduates do not attach to the crisis the meaning that has here been given it. Either they do not fear Hitler, or they fear war worse. Their general position is that of isolationists anywhere else in the country. If there is a crisis, they say, it is not in our effort to defend ourselves against Hitlerism but rather in our effort to keep out of the senseless carnage in Europe.

We all know the ins and outs of the long-winded and vigorous debate between the two groups that call each other isolationist and interventionist, and they need not concern us here. The debate is in any case somewhat spent and out-of-date, for there is not much left to intervene in, and we are increasingly aware that decisions about helping Britain must be made by military and naval experts on the cold hard ground of national security. We are in the war already; the question that remains is how to fight. But the various ideas which govern the thinking of contemporary young men have nowhere been more clearly illustrated than in that debate. In the colleges—and I am referring particularly to the early spring of 1940—there is plenty of time for talk and rather more frankness than you will find in Congress or the White House, and the discussion has been illuminating. It has brought out not only the superficial arguments about the vice or virtue of the French or British Empires, the strength or weakness of Hitler, the self-sufficiency or the international responsibilities of the United States; it has shown also the fundamental assumptions and attitudes from which in most cases these arguments have arisen. It is these basic beliefs that deserve our attention. They are the key to undergraduate thinking about America and the war. Where they are wrong, they are dangerously wrong, and where they are right they give a hope for the American future that is glowing, if none too certain. I shall deal mainly with the wrong ones. They are to be found among isolationists and interventionists both, and if the errors of the isolationist are more deep-seated and more immediately dangerous, those of the interventionist are more stupid and, in the long run, of equal importance. The isolationist errors may corrode our strength and deliver us helpless into the hands of the enemy; those of the interventionist may make our defense of no value, though it be outwardly successful.

Behind the great mass of undergraduate isolationist thinking are a number of assumptions which were almost unknown in the colleges of fifty years ago. They are modern, and they are, like most modern ideas, approximately half true. The half-truth is the most dangerous and effective form of lie. Of course there *are* isolationists who are not subject to these modern illusions, but they are very few, and they are particularly inconspicuous in the colleges. For the half-truths which I am about to discuss are very largely owned and operated by the educated youth of America.

The most obvious beliefs of contemporary isolationists arise out of the disappointing results of the last war. It is not astonishing that during the years of depression we all of us came to believe that war is a wholly destructive and undesirable phenomenon. It kills men, and those of us who read books like *The Horror of It* and *All Quiet on the Western Front* came early to the understanding that death in battle is seldom glorious or gay. War destroys property; it undermines institutions; it attacks the very ideals it purports to be defending. War is evil. This much is clearly true, and it is idiotic to think otherwise. What does not follow is the conclusion that war is at all costs to be avoided. For though war is evil, it is occasionally the lesser of two evils. But to a large majority of undergraduates and schoolboys in the years after 1929, it seemed impossible that anything could be worse than another war like that of 1914. And although the out-and-out pacifists were few—pacifism as a theory is somewhat too hard-and-fast for the "realism" on which we pride ourselves—those whose general attitude was peaceful were innumerable. This attitude made it difficult for us to believe people who spoke of Hitlerism as worse than war; it made us suspicious of people who continued to regard war as a potentially necessary instrument of national policy.

Even more important than our attitude toward war were the corollaries which, with the assistance of our elders, we drew from it. If war is bad, we reasoned, it follows that when we go to war it is for insufficient reasons. Turning to 1917, we found, or thought we found, that it was not idealism or any true sense of the national interest that took us in, but the machinations of the munitions-makers, the finaglings of the financiers, and the hysteria of a duped people. Here again we succumbed to a palpable half-truth, for if money and munitions and propaganda had their part in our decision then, still the decisive issues were the freedom of the seas and the German menace, which last was no less real for the fact that it was exaggerated. But we forgot about the justifiable causes of war in our concern over the profiteers and the propagandists. It was easier for us to do this than for people who lived through the last war, for we had never felt the idealism that moved Americans then; we knew Imperial Germany only as a failure whose crimes had been wildly overstated and whose Emperor was a pathetic old woodchopper. We had never felt the horrid fear of German victory, and when we complained about Versailles we never thought of Brest-Litovsk, for we saw it only as a dead letter.

So it was that in our thinking about foreign policy we worried more about keeping out of war than about the national security. And when war came to Europe again, we were concerned less with its meaning to us as a free people than with its effect on our bankers and our tear glands. Most of us were isolationists, and we pretended to ourselves that it made no difference who won, because if we allowed ourselves any sympathies we might make the worst of all mistakes and go to war. We opposed assistance to the Allies, because we did not want any cash nexus to drag us in. We treated the whole question as if this were the last war, and our version of that was based on an over-reading of *Road to War,* which had much more influence on the colleges than it had on Mr. Millis.

Since war to a good purpose seemed empirically impossible, it followed that those who wanted to lead us down the road to war were evil propagandists. "Perfidious Albion" is a phrase as well known here as in Europe, and the isolationists were ready to see Anglophile hysteria behind any and every argument for intervention. Dorothy Thompson, whose excitability has made her something of a joke on the campus, became the symbol of the kind of thinking we must avoid, and hardly anybody noticed how often Miss Thompson turned out to be right about Hitler, Chamberlain, and the folly of appeasement. This, thought the isolationists, is another imperialist struggle. It's all a matter of power politics; it must be, because war is bad, and you don't do bad things for a good reason.

If the prevailing opinion about the last war is the most powerful immediate influence on the isolationist, there are other broader attitudes which are basically more important. Not the least of these is the undergraduate's attitude toward what he is pleased to call *propaganda.*

The word "propaganda" has been desperately overworked by Americans in recent years. Everybody is worried about it, and nobody knows quite what it is. We have suddenly discovered that we can be influenced by a variety of irrelevant appeals; we have seen ourselves duped by advertisers and by politicians and by "sinister" or "subversive" forces, and the result is that we no longer know quite *what* to believe. And the colleges have the bug worst. This preoccupation with propaganda has its unfortunate effects, as we shall see, but it is not unmotivated or entirely unreasonable. Propaganda is too kind a word for some of the misinformation against which Americans must habitually guard themselves, and there is no more popular target of such propaganda than the growing child.

The old guard of this country, when they take it upon themselves to complain about the radical and corrupting influences of college teaching, complacently forget that the first source of youthful skepticism is the disillusionment that comes over us when our eyes are opened to the nonsense we have been taught by the righteous in our grammar school days. And if many college teachers overdo their insistence on detachment and independent thinking, they do so mainly because they are so eager to dislodge the prejudice and ignorance which have been carefully fostered by the schools and families of their students.

I remember clearly and somewhat painfully the first book of American history I read in grammar school. I read it swiftly and eagerly, for our history cannot be made dull by even the driest of historians, and this particular book (whose name I have mercifully forgotten) lost no chance to improve on reality. The Revolution was a series of triumphant victories against odds, spiced by patriotic comments on heroic fortitude and cowardly redcoats. Except for what appeared to be the conquest of the Louisiana territory, history then ceased until the war of 1812, in which we whipped the British navy and won the war at New Orleans. The story went on in like manner until in 1917 we had to go and win the World War, make the world safe for democracy, and to take our rank as the richest, wisest, bravest, kindest, strongest and most civilized of nations on the earth. Here the books of physical geography took up the story, and it became clear that we had more of everything than anybody else; history and geography taught us that man and nature had struggled since the dawn of time to produce the earthly Eden in which we found ourselves.

This is a great and astonishing country; it has a most remarkable history and an abundance of material blessings. But it has its weaknesses, and there are some imperfections in its past. To most Americans, brought up as they are to regard their country as more or less perfect, the discovery of these flaws comes as a shock. We are taught at an early age to salute the flag, to be patriotic, and to believe a lot of lies. It is therefore not surprising that when our eyes are opened, we react rather strongly against the innocent credulity of our childhood. I remember wondering a little, when I first studied American history, at my mother's lack of interest in the Daughters of the American Revolution, to membership in which her ancestry entitles her; it seemed to me that she was rather cold and unpatriotic about it all. As I learned more, I understood better; I forgave my mother and tried to forget the D.A.R. When one's first steps in patriotism turn out to be misguided, it is only natural that one should become a skeptic. The professional patriots have only themselves to blame if they find American youth unsympathetic. Once bitten, twice shy.

Our disillusionment in the field of American history is typical of others that we have known, in our religion, in our politics, and in our attitudes toward all kinds of institutions and ideas. These disappointments, and the results that have come of them, are significant in more ways than one. But for the present we must confine ourselves to the question of propaganda. People who have repeatedly seen the cloak of righteousness covering the knave and the fool are inclined to be suspicious about all righteousness everywhere. And as our schooling advanced, most of us came in contact with teachers and writers not at all reluctant to teach us the ways of the wary. Our knowledge of the propaganda of the last war is at least as extensive as our understanding of its battles and politics. We know about the "slanting" of news in the papers; we mistrust all columnists and orators. Were it not for the fact that there is money in it, and respectable citizens to boot, we should be inclined to regard advertising as the lowest of trades. We have been taught about propaganda, and the lesson has been well learned.

The worst critic of youth can hardly blame it for a fear of propaganda. We are right to be careful; the trouble is that our caution often leads us to confusion and foolishness. If you approach everything as propaganda, you become far less concerned about the arguments that are advanced than with the motives of the people advancing them. If a man makes a convincing speech about, say, the advisability of helping the British, you can consider his arguments answered if you identify him as an habitual Anglophile. An overweening concern about propaganda leads to a retreat from reason and to *argumentum ad hominem*. In this most unfortunate tendency undergraduates are encouraged by the amateurish smattering of modern psychology with which they are provided. They know all about rationalization, and they consider it far more prevalent than reason. They are probably right, but to discard reason because much reasoning is bad is like discarding Christianity because some ministers are morons. (Undergraduates are much given, incidentally, to this second practice.)

Mistrust of reason and fear of propaganda are apparent in much isolationist thought. Not only does the average hardened isolationist bury all opposing arguments in the category of partisan propaganda; he refuses to admit to himself the most obvious facts on the ground that they will unreasonably sway him. Thus, as Professor Arnold Whitredge recently remarked in the *Atlantic,* the Nazi invasions of small neutrals went undenounced by the isolationist editor of the *Yale News,* while the rescue of the *Altmark* prisoners was roundly cursed as British lawlessness. What it comes down to is this: the isolationist's fear of false evidence favoring the British leads him to a denial of any evidence that tends in the same direction. This is emphatically not the result of any conscious dishonesty. It comes rather of confused thinking. But the French politicians and generals who failed to save their country were not dishonest; they simply didn't understand. The honesty of the isolationist will not make his confusions less dangerous.

The puzzled graduates of Yale who do not understand undergraduate isolationism have often asked why it is that these obstinate young people are not upset by the outrages of Hitler, and why, further, they respond so feebly to the moral issues involved in the present war. There are many, many answers to these questions, but one of the most important is directly related to the attitudes we have just been discussing. Hitler's outrages are well understood in the colleges, and it is doubtful if there is any group in the country more deeply and bitterly opposed to the way of life he represents. Undergraduates have seen the real evils of Hitlerism since 1933, and it is notable that often the very people who are now isolationists were once found among the most vocal of his enemies. The trouble is that now, when there is some danger of our being dragged into war (remember that war has been painted to us as the greatest possible evil), people who talk about the beast of Berlin seem like propagandists for intervention. Their words are reminiscent of the exaggerated tales about the Huns which we have seen exposed since 1918. And so the undergraduate, while no lover of the Nazis, prefers not to listen to stories of their wickedness or of their designs in South America. It is a case of "Wolf, Wolf"; the isolationist does not think the Huns were a real menace in the last war, and now that the real thing is here, he will not recognize it because it looks so much like a fake.

The supposed indifference of undergraduates toward the moral issues can be largely explained in the same way. It is true that we rise slowly and suspiciously to the bait of glowing generalities. The terms in which I have stated my belief in opposing Hitlerism would be dismissed by most young isolationists as abstract nothings. Partly the difficulty lies deeper than any fear of propaganda and relates to a still more important attitude which we have yet to discuss. But much of the trouble comes simply from the fact that the undergraduate has seen so many different people taking refuge in the same noble phrases that idealistic abstractions must be very carefully and cogently expressed before he will pay any attention. The economists have their Gresham's Law, to the effect that bad money drives out good. There is a similar law in language; if any given word, say "democracy," is sufficiently misused, it will cease to have any valuable meaning. So long as countless demagogues and idiots go hog-calling with the most important abstract nouns in the language, it will be difficult for any man to speak with great effect about truth and freedom and law and idealism. The undergraduate isolationist is taking no chances, and it is not hard for him to believe that all these words mean as little when applied to the struggle against Hitler as they mean when Hearst and Mayor Kelly apply them to Messrs. Willkie and Roosevelt respectively. Because he knows how often professions of idealism are utterly worthless, the undergraduate prefers not to talk about "moral issues" and "basic beliefs." It is understandable, this attitude, but unfortunately when a real moral issue comes along, it is disastrous not to recognize it. This is true in personal morality, where the same misguided realism often leads young

Americans to unhappiness they scarcely deserve, and it is true also in the morality of government and of foreign policy. We are wise to be careful about propaganda, but not everything is propaganda. It is easier to believe nothing than to sift out the truth from a great pile of distorted facts and camouflaged lies. But people who disregard reality, however plausible their reasons for doing so, are not really any wiser than the dupes at whom they sneer.

Their feelings about war and propaganda are powerful contributing factors to the isolationist stand of the undergraduates, but there is a still more important and general attitude, which underlies so much of undergraduate thinking that by its very prevalence it often escapes notice. Back of our disillusionment with war, back of our fear of propaganda, is *a deep-seated uncertainty about all ideals and every absolute.*

As we have already observed, the policy advocated in this book involves extensive sacrifices, in time and money, and possibly in blood. To support such a policy a man must either be blind to what he is doing or he must have something fairly precious to fight for. Nobody ever willingly faces war except in the service of an ideal. There are economic causes of war, of course, and they are important, but the individual citizen will rarely fight for bread or gold alone. Certainly the contemporary undergraduate will not do so, for he knows that modern war is inevitably and in all cases destructive of wealth. It follows, therefore, that without ideals no undergraduate will nowadays fight at all, unless he be forced. The policy we have advocated is not only opposed to Hitlerism, but vigorously and aggressively opposed; it must correspondingly be supported by a fighting faith, or not at all. And fighting faith is not prevalent among contemporary college men. About the things for which we are willing to die, we are confused and bewildered; we have played with many ideals, but we have generally given our devotion to none.

The proper understanding of this matter is absolutely essential to any discussion of the thinking of youth; it is the most disquieting single aspect of the undergraduate scene, and it arises from a combination of influences so widespread that it can fairly be said that every one is to be blamed for it—educators of all sorts, ministers, parents, and the undergraduates themselves. It is because any critic feels a duty to excuse his own group that the people who talk about "the trouble with young people" generally present an analysis that is hopelessly distorted. In order to avoid any such distortion, I shall myself presently concede a few undergraduate weaknesses, but it is more convenient and more comfortable to start with other sinners.

There is a story told around New Haven which well illustrates the difficulties in which an innocent and idealistic young man finds himself when thrown on the not very tender mercies of a college faculty. A hot-headed Virginia Freshman, annoyed to find an instructor in psychology proctoring a test, indignantly remarked to the proctor that such precautions were unnecessary, because "I, suh, am a Southern Christian gentleman." To which the proctor replied, "In other words, sir, you are environmentally overconditioned, emotionally unbalanced, and a victim of bourgeois ideology." A Yankee like myself is still sufficiently aware of the Civil War to be mildly pleased by a rebel's discomfiture, but it is not very funny for a more or less defenseless youngster to have three of his most cherished ideals put on the same plane as a case of measles. And the remarks of this probably nonexistent instructor are representative of a great deal of university teaching. An objective and analytical approach is of course essential to all proper scholarly investigation, and it is easy to understand the impatience of the teacher confronted by a student who apparently brings to a simple problem no better equipment than a bundle of prejudices. At the same time, even a Northerner can see the greatness of the Southern tradition, anyone but a fool can see that Christianity is not a subject for light raillery, and the concept of the gentleman is rather older and more honorable than many of the concepts of Karl Marx.

The searching study to which scholarship has subjected all of man's feelings and most of his works has produced many valuable results. But a little learning is even more dangerous nowadays than it was in the time of Pope; and the instruction which knocks out "ignorant superstition" and fails to put anything in its place is probably worse than no instruction at all.

Examples of unfortunate if well-intentioned teaching can be found in almost every field. The scientist who says that there is no truth save the truth of exact science is making an observation that is strictly accurate, in a limited sense; there is a special validity about the results of a chemical experiment that can never be attached to any conclusion in the humanities. But if the scientist allows his students to conclude that the physical sciences have the inside track to all reality, he is guilty of the most dangerous sort of special pleading. Nothing leads more surely to frustration than the attempt to treat human truth as scientific truth; there are thousands of young Americans who have nothing to live by, because they want to live by scientific truth, which as yet gives no dependable directions for the Good Life.

Then there is the historian who must present in class a complete and accurate picture of the way of life of a given people in a given century. Such a man, honest and intelligent, learned and human, may avoid all the lesser errors to which historians are prone—he may give economics its just place, and no more; he may intertwine religion and politics, thought and action, ideas and things into a whole which shows no sign of prejudiced or unbalanced treatment. But if he cannot make his students come alive to a true understanding of those people in that century, he has failed. If he has taught them to think of the religion of the time, or the political principles, as buttons which can be pressed in order to grind out explanations of this or that occurrence, he has driven one more nail into the coffin which contains the undergraduate soul. For if you think always dispassionately about beliefs which were of life-and-death importance to the men that held them, if you understand revolution or religious conflict with your head and not your heart, you are well on your way to the loss of your own convictions. An eternally objective attitude toward others leads eventually to the decay of one's own faith.

But the historian and the scientist, even at their worst, are innocent in comparison with the social scientist, not because the social scientist has a more devilish nature, but because his opportunities for the devil's work are much more numerous. It is his business to pry into the workings of our own contemporary society and to show us why we think and act as we do; this is a perfectly legitimate trade. It is not necessary for us to be the less Christian for knowing more or less why we are Christian or the less law-abiding for knowing why we have laws. But when a man like Thurman Arnold, recently attached to my own university, has made his analysis of *The Symbols of Government* or *The Folklore of Capitalism,* you feel like a fool for having respected the Supreme Court or honored the law or considered a principle as anything better than a tool. Mr. Arnold differs from his colleagues in that he is more deliberately cynical and somewhat sharper of tongue than most, but of the prevailing influence in the colleges he is unpleasantly representative. I freely concede that such books as his are entertaining and even instructive. Mr. Arnold and others do a real service when they point out that plenty of fine phrases are shibboleths and plenty of fond beliefs unjustified. But the remarkable discovery that even a Supreme Court justice is human does not justify the conclusion that there is no such thing as government by law. The case of the debunkers is ludicrously overstated; but because it is striking, entertaining, and about half true, it is popular.

The predicament in which a man is placed when he accepts this point of view can be understood if we consider the curious logical difficulty of Mr. Arnold's own benevolent cynicism. Mr. Arnold apparently has at heart a number of noble objectives. He would not call them noble, but that doesn't matter; it is clear that he regards himself as a man of good will. But he also regards himself as a realist, and he therefore dismisses as meaningless most of the popular concepts of virtue. He is concerned in a strictly practical fashion with the greatest good of the greatest number; honesty, justice, and humanitarianism are a lot of useless mouthings. Now in point of fact Mr. Arnold probably has a perfectly orthodox personal attitude toward these mouthings and neither cheats at poker nor beats his dog. But observe the difficulty in which he finds himself: having denied the relevance of morality in politics, how is he to judge between one form of government and another, except in terms of its material results? He condemns Hitler and Mussolini as intolerant rulers, and probably he hates the Nazis as much as any of us. But his own announced position makes it impossible for him to point out any essential difference between us and Hitler, except that Hitler's energies run more to armies, a difference which would disappear if the submissions of the British and ourselves made it possible for Hitler to turn to "peaceful domination." "Intolerance," Mr. Arnold, is a moralistic mouthing. And if Mr. Arnold himself has sufficient mental agility to be undamaged by his own foolishness, he and teachers like him have many honest and innocent followers who find themselves extremely confused when they try to treat a truly moral issue on the purely practical level.

The faculties of our colleges have thus succeeded, often unintentionally, in making a very good case against the idealism and faith without which no settled way of life can be maintained in a crisis. And their words have not fallen on unresponsive ears. The undergraduate is remarkably weakly attached to any tradition or any creed, and it is not hard to cut him loose from what little he has. The thinking in college is often clever and almost always honest, but it is seldom disciplined or cautious or profound. The undergraduate has a lamentable tendency to believe that the new view must be the true view. We are remarkably impatient of advice from our elders, believing as we do that we are much better able than they to see the new truth and understand the modern world. Because the world has changed very rapidly in its externals, and because therefore we are in many of the little things more worldly wise than those who grew up thirty years ago, we are inclined to pretend to a knowledge of the big things which we are very far from having. We often forget that an understanding of cocktails and automobiles does not imply any particular understanding of good and evil. We fall swiftly and easily for "modern" ideas, and nothing is more modern than a critical and suspicious attitude toward the various ideals which have in the past been the inspiration of most Americans.

The basic lack of faith of the average undergraduate expresses itself in a great variety of specific opinions, almost all of which lend support to the isolationist position. There is the attitude of the man who identifies his own confusion and unhappiness with the state of the nation at large. He thinks somewhat as follows: "There is nothing worth fighting for, because I can't find it. There's no job, no religion, nobody loves me, democracy is a hoax. Maybe Hitler is right after all, and anyhow we aren't sure he isn't, so why pretend we are and get into a bloody mess over nothing?" Or there is the person who honestly disapproves of the Nazis and yet cannot justify to himself any vigorous opposition to them. He knows that he doesn't want to live Hitler's way, but he doesn't think he has a right to make momentous decisions on a shadowy and rather abstract basis. He remembers that life, after all, still goes on in Germany, and if it is different, the difference is mainly in ideals and purposes, which are, he believes, of no real significance. Thirdly, there is the individual who avows himself a democrat and a Christian and yet persists in judging democracy and Christianity on a purely material basis. To such a one it seems preposterous to talk of the righteousness of defending a country which has ten million unemployed and a thousand and one pressing economic problems. He can see nothing in democracy and Christianity that is not measured in terms of "efficiency" and "security." Talk to him of the dignity of the individual or the freedom guaranteed in the Constitution, talk to him of the elementary right of free speech and free thought, and he pays no attention. These are abstractions, and he will never know how real they are unless some day he finds he hasn't got them.

It is the men who think along these lines that form the really dangerous American fifth column, without realizing it. They are thinking exactly as the Nazis would wish them to think, and their cooperation with Hitler is the more effective for being quite unconscious. A nation cannot be stronger or more devoted to its own ideals than the people who compose it. Nazi Germany, whatever its crimes, and whatever the suffering and the mental slavery of its inhabitants, has the priceless advantage of unity of faith. Hitler is an arch-villain, but he has armies that will die for him and a people whose morale improves with each success. National Socialism is a fighting faith. Against a people who are confused and materialistic and unsure of their own ideals, it will inevitably conquer, as it has against overwhelming odds in Europe since 1932.

We must not leave the subject of the undermined faith of young Americans without commenting on two other important aspects of it, the roles that have been played by the men who tried to prevent it and by the economic depression. The majority of ministers, teachers, and fathers are deeply disturbed by the apathy of youth in the face of moral and spiritual issues, and yet it is largely through their own blunders that this apathy has developed. They have made, in most cases, one or the other of two fatal errors. Either they have overstated their case, or they have not stated it at all. In the former case, they seem stupid and contemptible, for nothing more annoys an undergraduate than bogus idealism; the minister who preaches of a world of sweetness and light and a nation united in brotherly love is talking nonsense, and the undergraduate, whatever his other failings, is not a sentimentalist. Nor is it wise for a minister to dodge the tough parts of his creed as if theology were an intellectual fifth wheel to the religious coach; the undergraduate wants a faith that combines intelligence with feeling. In the same way, he scorns unreasoned patriotism and the bland complacence that preaches of America as the land of progress, plenty, virtue and happiness. The term *Boy Scout* is one of derision in the colleges, not because the Scouts of America are not an excellent organization, but because so many Pollyannas have taken it upon themselves to praise the Scout movement for virtues that do not exist except in heaven. Many an undergraduate feels that his choice must be between the clumsy stupidity of the professional optimist and the cynicism of complete disbelief; and if these really were his alternatives, I at least should be on the side of the cynic. For in a choice between two forms of futility the more entertaining is always preferable.

But most of our elders are not guilty of this kind of foolishness. Aware of our aversion to moralizing, and honoring what they recognize as our wish to find our way alone, they keep their own counsel about basic principles and fundamental ideals. In some cases, of course, this is because they haven't got any conscious principles; in others they suffer from an inability to communicate intelligently their very definite beliefs. But generally they are silent because they think we want them to be silent, and they are right. Certainly the domineering parent is almost always an unsuccessful one. Nevertheless it is extremely unfortunate that many men of real wisdom and feeling are serene in a mistaken belief that the younger generation will safely work out its own salvation. At least our elders need not conceal from us the fact that they themselves have found certain beliefs and standards compellingly valid and even indispensable. For we look to older people more than we are willing to admit, and though we reject advice, we profit by example. A teacher or father who deliberately conceals his strongest convictions in order that he may not unduly influence the young is in fact guilty of unduly influencing them toward an absence of conviction. For they know him, they think, quite well; they like him; in spite of themselves they take him a little as a standard; and he appears to have no strong beliefs. There are any number of courses at Yale which a student can attend for a year without ever hearing a syllable about the personal attitude of the lecturer toward the things he is discussing. Only one man among the nineteen under whom I studied at Yale ever really opened his heart in a class and showed me the stuff of his convictions; to that man I feel a personal debt that I cannot begin to estimate. A number of my courses were in such subjects as mathematics and theoretical economics, and I concede the difficulty of making a moral issue of a semicubical parabola; but mainly I worked in the humanities, and although many of my instructors were brilliant and almost all of them sincere scholars, they never really let themselves go. Our elders complain about our reticence in discussing ideals; their own reticence is at least as great, and yet surely on their own estimate of the relative wisdom of the two generations, it is more important for them than for us to be outspoken.

If the men of conviction in the older generation have in my opinion been too little blamed for their share of the confusion of youth, I am convinced that our economic difficulties, to which we have laid almost every trouble of the last decade, have been unjustly pilloried as the major cause of youth's disillusionment. It is often said that if we wish men to believe in democracy, we must make democracy work, and when people talk about making democracy work they are thinking in terms of material success. According to this view, democracy is always at the mercy of economics, and depends for its maintenance upon a constantly increasing measure of material security. This is still another half-truth, for if it is true that no free society can maintain its stability in the face of starvation and hopeless poverty, it is true also that neither boundless wealth nor complete individual security can guarantee the "democratic way." Though an economically unsuccessful society will be doubted and even attacked by those whom it mistreats, it is utterly wrong to believe that our way is better than Hitler's only if it will make us richer. And while I cannot speak for the broad mass of youth, I am quite sure that the undergraduates of this country have been made more thoughtful and less self-satisfied, but not more cynical and less hopeful, by the depression. I know that there are so-called youth leaders who clamor that *Youth* wants jobs and is becoming desperate in enforced idleness, and certainly unemployment among the young is a serious problem. It is, however, a notable fact that in general these youth leaders are talking not about themselves but about some other youth, for most youth leaders are extremely busy people. It is absolutely without sarcasm that I am inclined to point at the youth leaders themselves as examples of the change of attitude caused by the depression. Their ideas seem to me mostly wrong, and I regard the American Youth Congress as an excellent place in which to watch at work most of the attitudes I have been attacking, but it is nevertheless important to recognize that the members of the Congress seem to be neither fools nor men of little faith. Their mistaken attitudes do not include cynicism or doubt. The depression has of course shaken the faith of a few young men; there are people, as I have already remarked, who consider economic failure a proof of the decadence of both God and America. But a faith which depends on security and material success is of little value in any case, and I think the depression's most important effect on our individual ideals has been to open our eyes to the fruitlessness of a life that is based on the calculus of comfort. This is certainly true in the colleges, where the undergraduate of 1940 is more serious, more discerning, and much more of a real idealist than his counterpart of 1929.

We have used the term "faith" in a somewhat general sense, as the basis of conviction without which honest men have no reason to make great sacrifices. The essential difficulty of American youth is that, having learned the weakness but not the strength of the creeds of their fathers, they have been unable to find their own way to an acceptance of any ideal. Full of good will, and honestly eager to know the truth, they are paralyzed by their own unfortunate confusions. Where the young Nazi has seen his wretchedly perverted ideal winning one success after another and has thus not unnaturally become more and more frantically attached to it, the young American, who leans over backwards to be honest, has been forced to concede failure on failure in the creed he would rather like to accept and has been taught to forget that right is not made wrong by failure. Paraphrasing Richard II, an American undergraduate might well summarize his own difficulties and the advantages of the Nazi in the following couplet:

> My faith is lack of faith, by old faith done;
> Your faith is gain of faith, by new faith won.

And unless we take energetic measures to change this situation, we are likely to find ourselves in a position very much like that of the unhappy Richard. The Nazis, like Bolingbroke, are not beaten by words. They can be stopped only by a vigilance and energy that do not come from the half-hearted or the unconvinced. We must be able to paraphrase Shakespeare still again and say

> Your faith set up does not pluck my faith down.

So far we have been discussing attitudes of mind which for one reason or another are more conspicuous in the colleges than in other parts of the country. Hatred of war, fear of propaganda, and lack of faith are not, however, the only contributing causes of undergraduate isolationism. There are others which, while they are no more prevalent in the colleges than elsewhere, should briefly be considered. These other factors can be lumped together as a preoccupation with things that any defense effort, particularly if it leads to war, will endanger. Thus there are isolationists who get that way because they are all wrapped up in their own plans, their own health, prosperity, peace, and security. All of these things are more or less endangered by a vigorous foreign policy. There are isolationists who are worried about civil liberties and democracy in time of war; observing quite rightly that militarism is not friendly to individual rights, they conclude that the best thing to do is to avoid militarism and war, at almost any price. There are isolationists whose major motivation is a preoccupation with the cause of labor; there are others who see in isolation the one chance of preserving free industry and the rights of capital.

All those who allow perfectly legitimate objectives to become an argument for isolation are the victims of an understandable but very dangerous shortsightedness. Their error is precisely the error that so many Europeans have made since 1933. They are unable to see that the most dangerous enemy of their special interest is Hitlerism; they avoid the lesser evil and thus lay themselves open to the greater one. They are making the same old mistakes; they are the people who must listen to Miss Mann. Her words have the telling effect of bitter first-hand experience; their lesson is a simple one: don't spend your time shutting windows when the front door is wide open. Which is worse, conscription or submission? (I am at a loss to understand the folk who argue that conscription is equivalent to fascism. I seem to remember it as a practice of democratic France, and democratic Switzerland; one might almost as well argue that a policeman and a gangster are identical because they both carry guns.) Was France more or less free as a fighting democracy than she is today? And where are the business men and workers at this moment better off, in England or in Germany? This is no ordinary enemy we face. The price of resistance is high, but the price of nonresistance is higher.

Working singly or in combination, the various attitudes I have discussed are to be found behind the arguments of almost every isolationist, and I am sure that it is the attitudes and not the arguments which must be overcome. A man who assumes that war is the worst of evils must be shown that his assumption is basically wrong before he will listen to arguments in favor of a policy that has in it implicitly a willingness to fight if necessary. A man who has the propaganda bug will not listen to any arguments at all until you can convince him of your good faith and of his obligation at least to listen to you. A man without faith cannot be told straight out that it is worthwhile to make sacrifices for this, that or the other ideal; he must first be convinced that idealism actually exists as something more than a term of reproach. And a man who is preoccupied with other things will not be concerned with the Nazi menace unless you can show him either that his other interests are unworthy or that the Nazis are the worst existing threat to them. To any reader who has rejected the main thesis of this book, I respectfully suggest a searching of his own soul, to see if one or another of these attitudes does not possess an unjustifiable hold upon him. I have never yet argued at any length with an isolationist without finding that his mind turned back time and again to one or more of them. They have formed the basis for more wishful thinking than all the peaceful promises of Hitler. And they have only a little more validity.

On the most pressing and vital immediate issue, the isolationist is terribly wrong, but on many important matters his views are a good deal more accurate than those of the opposition. The services of the isolationist have therefore been extremely valuable in tempering the wild-eyed hysteria to which Americans are subject when they face a national crisis. Among undergraduates at least there are very few who have not felt the force of the attitudes described above, so that even those who have discarded isolationism are still aware of those parts of isolationist doctrine which are clearly and completely right. For this reason the errors of the interventionist, potentially of the gravest danger, have thus far been kept more or less in check. Against *these* errors the isolationist attitudes are a very strong guarantee. As our energies are more and more taken up in the crisis, however, the popular appeal of these other fallacies will increase, and we shall find it hard to avoid them. The truth of our situation is neither simple nor one-sided, but people who have a desperately serious job to do are seldom eager to remember its complexities. In compensation for the attacks I have made on the isolationists, I am therefore driven to point out the pitfalls into which we on our side are prone to fall. These "interventionists' errors" fall quite naturally into the same four categories as those of their opponents, mistakes about war, mistakes about propaganda, about ideals, and about secondary purposes.

The fact that war is on occasion an indispensable instrument of national policy does not mean that war is any better than

Sherman said it was. The generations since Sherman have in fact devoted a large part of their effort to the creation of machines and tactics that make the hellishness of 1864 seem almost tame. It is therefore extremely distressing to find an increasing number of amiable young zealots rather discounting the evils of modern war. Not only do they overemphasize the glory of the thing, but they incline in some mysterious fashion to believe that national defense is just a matter of voting money and hiring brilliant business men and gamboling around an amateurish training camp. They treat the nation's armament program as rather a lark, and they do not trouble themselves with its grim meaning. They complacently ignore the fact that our defense effort will have to have some quite unpleasant aspects if it is to be successful; its influence on every one of us and on all our domestic interests will be profound and, if we are not careful, very dangerous. A program like the one Congress and the country have undertaken is not begun in fun, and people who accept it without a serious study of its meaning are going to do and say things that are both stupid and destructive.

Propaganda has not yet been seriously misunderstood by the interventionists, largely because they have so far not had a free hand in manufacturing and misusing it. But already one hears remarks which foreshadow the mistakes to come. It is said, for example, that if national defense is a necessity, it is rather unwise to publicize its economic costs; certainly, we are told, there should be no admission of any minor weaknesses in our own country or any minor accomplishments of the Germans. This attitude is utterly damnable; it has not, in my opinion, any of the redeeming virtues of the isolationist errors. It is neither intelligent nor honest, and these are two of the most conspicuous qualities of the average isolationist. (If I were to attempt a generalization on the subject of the typical isolationist, I should describe him as a man of unquestionable integrity with a strongly analytical mind and a rather feeble sense of general human values; my own isolationist friends, with a couple of exceptions, conform quite remarkably to this general frame.) It gives me some comfort that thus far this type of interventionist thinking seems to be very rare among undergraduates. We are sufficiently aware of the things for which America must be defended not to countenance any form of lying or deceit as a weapon of defense. We know that such weapons are destructive in the long run; we realize also that they are of very little use. The American people are strong enough to hear the truth, and they will kick up a pretty mess if anybody tries to play George Creel's game again. We have reached a stage of public enlightenment when the one best weapon of the propagandist is the unvarnished truth. The brilliant success of Winston Churchill as a leader of democracy in a crisis can be largely attributed to the candor with which he speaks to Parliament and his nation. So it is devoutly to be hoped that interventionists will always base their own beliefs and their appeals to others on fact and not fancy. There are plenty of facts, after all.

The question of faith, or ultimate understanding of the issues at hand, is of course the most significant of the four categories we are discussing. It is in this matter that mistakes are most dangerous, on both sides. And though the interventionist cannot be accused of a lack of faith, since he is generally a strong believer in the set of ideals which Hitler's world revolution denies, he may easily fall into a scarcely less dangerous delusion. Believing that only a firm stand against Hitler can safeguard the things in which he believes, he finds it quite natural to equate a successful defense against Hitler with the triumph of his ideals, thus unconsciously committing a simple error in logic. If we are to protect our ideals, we must stop Hitler, but it does not follow that if we stop Hitler, our ideals will be safe. There are a good many dangers to our principles which have nothing to do with Hitler's revolution, and there are others which will arise out of our very opposition to Hitler. It is therefore entirely wrong to believe that we best serve our ideals by devoting every ounce of energy to any and every operation which works to the frustration of mad Adolf. It would make us stronger, possibly, to suspend the November election and to imprison all those who do not like Mr. Roosevelt's face. But it would not serve our real purposes. The necessities of defense will almost surely force us to actions not entirely consonant with our ideas of the American way, but we must see to it that only necessities have this effect on us. The man who believes that the military security of this country is our one great object is making an error remarkably like that of the patriotic Germans who support Hitler as the Nation's savior. Guns, ships, tanks and planes are all important; so are men trained to use them. But these things are our servants; it will be a fatal mistake to treat them as an end in themselves. This mistake is as yet being made by very few younger people, but militarism is in its way dramatic, and only clear heads and sound hearts will keep us wholly safe from its temptations.

It is largely because of their error in faith that so many interventionists make the mistakes they do in considering the various aspects of domestic life that are affected by an extensive program of defense. If national defense is its own justification, incidental injuries done to labor, industry, civil liberties, and the spirit of the people become quite unimportant. Already voices are being raised in an attempt to crush the labor movement on the pretext of national emergency, and similar voices are heard from the other side remarking that now is the time to finish off the vested interests. Still others call for a suspension of such elementary American liberties as free speech and free assembly. Not only are such suggestions quite unjustified by national necessity, but they contribute to a state of mind which will make the nation's defense vastly more difficult. Workers or employers who seek to take advantage of the crisis will be bitterly opposed, and the resulting struggle will weaken us all. Honest compromise, a sort of temporary truce, is the only possible solution of the problem; any attempt to make a good thing out of the crisis will merely turn to civil strife energies that are needed for a united effort.

As for civil liberties and the Bill of Rights, they must not be suspended under any circumstances. It is one thing to be firm toward fifth columnists and quite another to suspend the ordinary rights of ordinary Americans. I myself do not include members of the Communist Party or the German-American Bund in the category of ordinary Americans; it seems to me perfectly evident that both groups are essentially owned and controlled by unscrupulous foreign governments; this is a vexed issue, largely because so many people cannot see the difference between a Communist and other types of Leftist, but the facts of Communist action and thought speak clearly for themselves, and the Bund is obviously as much at Hitler's disposal as the German army. Even in these cases, however, we must proceed by law and with restraint. The Constitution contains no justification of treachery, however subtle; it is our business to distinguish carefully between traitors and people we don't happen to like. The inevitable stringencies of a military emergency must be kept at an absolute minimum, and unfortunately there is no formula that can do it for us. The tension between civil rights and military necessity cannot be resolved by rule of thumb. We must therefore rely on our judges, our administrators, and on our whole people, to show the wisdom and discernment without which we shall unreasonably multiply dangers and difficulties which are quite large enough already.

We have been considering mistakes we must not make; it is now high time for a more positive discussion. Crises like the present one are not victoriously resolved by people who merely avoid mistakes. There are heavy tasks facing us all, and no one has a higher responsibility than the undergraduates of American colleges. I can think of no other way to conclude this chapter than by a summary of the things that I would have us do.

Our first job is to understand and accept our obligations as men of independent mind. We have assumed the right to do our own thinking, to find our own God, to accept or reject any and every belief, to take nothing on the say-so of our elders. In this declaration of independence we are justified only if we carry out for ourselves the function we have denied to others. Though we will not be bludgeoned into belief, we are bound to make most earnest efforts to understand and judge fairly the various beliefs to which our elders urge us. Nobody has much right to life, let alone education, if he is not willing to seek out the fundamental purpose, the ultimate ideal, toward which he lives. We have got to find the Good, and we have got to be brave enough to make our acceptance of the Good an act of faith. Neither good nor evil, for all the refined sophistry of professors of ethics, can be proved; we must nevertheless believe that both of them exist, on higher levels and in broader terms than those of the pickpocket or the card cheat.

Having made this first and most important step, we must move on to the hard work which so many earnest believers ignore. It is uncommonly consoling to have found the Truth, and uncommonly easy to be neither honest nor intelligent about Its implications. It is here, in the task of "thinking things through," that college men have a special opportunity for service. To see clearly the real stakes, to be wary of propaganda but not blind to fact, to fight against evil, without malice and yet without weakness—these must be our aims; their fulfillment, as I have tried to show, is both important and difficult. I make no claims for the undergraduate as a person of perfect wisdom; he has lived lightheartedly for many years, and like other Americans he is unprepared for the jobs that must now be done. He is ignorant and undisciplined in mind, confused and slightly atrophied in spirit. But he has the raw materials of greatness. He is intelligent, honest, fearless and warmhearted.

But wisdom cannot be produced overnight; it is like a two-ocean navy or a baby, swiftly conceived but slowly and painfully delivered. And it is here that I find the real task of the undergraduate today. He can be shown how to shoot a gun; his military training is a problem to be handled by military men. But his mind and heart are in his own keeping; for them he has sole responsibility, and neither teacher nor minister, speech nor book, can do for him what he will not do for himself. For laziness and superficiality, for ignorance and stupidity, for all the mistakes that study and thought and self-discipline can avert, the undergraduate beyond other men can be held to strict accountability. He is his own biggest job.

It is odd, in a way, that this chapter should end in an appeal for the simple personal virtue of self-discipline. And yet such a conclusion is quite proper. The aim of men like Hitler is to destroy men's freedom; the Nazis have done their best to sweep away every safeguard man has built for the protection of his most precious possession—his own soul. If their revolution sweeps the world, by conquest and by internal decay, there will be no need for self-discipline, for no man will any longer be his own ruler. We have won in this country the right to live as men, not slaves—more accurately, this right was won for us, long ago, and has been maintained more by chance than by vigilance. Now we face a time of trial; the immediate danger is from Berlin, but the general threat is not localized in place or limited in time. Whatever the outcome of the war in Europe, the attack will be prolonged and energetic. And the test for us is simple; as individuals controlling our own souls, can we find that wisdom and the courage to defend successfully our individual freedom? We may act as citizens of a nation or as soldiers of an alliance, but basically we are defending our own personal domain. And that most intimate and important kingdom can be defended only if it is well ruled. We shall find neither wisdom nor strength without an effort, and each man must make the effort for himself.

"Laws, freedom, truth, and faith in God"—these, as beautifully summarized by the hymn-writer, are the ideals of America. They are complex in their application, though simple in their conception, and we know that they are all under fire. Our job, then, is to defend them. Each of them is a bulwark of our dignity as men. Each of them is precious beyond any of the truths of science or any of the comforts of a bathtub civilization. To understand them, to understand their enemies, to work wisely and well in their defense, these are the duties of civilized Americans. We shall be faced with many evils, and the lesser evil will often be our only possible choice. In such trying circumstances, we shall need men who have brains, guts, and hearts, all in good condition.

I have written in this chapter of the errors that I find in the thinking of my contemporaries; in these things I may be wrong. I have written also of the responsibility of the individual for his own best development as a man of knowledge and conviction; in this I am surely right. So I hope that the American graduate will face the difficult future with the tempered mind and the disciplined affections that mark a really free man. The colleges and universities of this country are almost the last in the world which can freely pursue their search for truth. They are the living symbols of a way of thought that is now desperately in danger. It will be a nasty irony if in the face of this danger the college and university men are found among those who look the other way. And if, in an hour of defeat, they turn desperately against the enemy they have underestimated, it will not help them that their errors were natural enough and their intentions honorable.

But that hour has not yet come, and it need never come. This extraordinary country can be limited in its future only by the limits of the vision and wisdom of its citizens. So the issue rests with each one of us. If we will fight our way to the truth, if we will insist on living in the light, we shall be well able to handle the things that live in darkness and are fed on lies. The challenge is in the word *if*.

IV

I SAW IT HAPPEN

William L. White

IV

I SAW IT HAPPEN

I

This chapter is presumably addressed to youth in relation to Europe, but I shall lead off with a nice old lady who sat down to write me, with shaky handwriting, to the effect that she thinks under no circumstances should we ever let our boys face shot and shell on foreign soil. And I won't argue with her, except to point out that in this she differs from the equally nice old ladies of Europe who have recently seen a good deal of war, usually from the vantage point of a two-wheeled cart, perched on their household belongings, holding a parrot cage in one hand and a couple of squirming kids under the other arm, and occasionally jumping down to crouch under a culvert when an enemy plane dives to go rat-tat-tat-tat along the road.

Now I think my nice old American lady, if she could talk to some of these nice old European ladies whose handwriting, by this time, is even more shaky than hers, would presently get their point of view. It is that wars are a lot more fun for everybody concerned, including nice old ladies, if it can be arranged so that they will be fought on the soil of some country other than your own. The nice old ladies of Germany are properly grateful to Hitler because he arranged it so that the hand grenades would go off in someone else's jam closet and crack someone else's cookie jars, rather than their own. This also goes for the nice, kindly old gentlemen of Germany who, when they mislay their spectacles, can at least be sure they aren't buried under a couple of cubic metres of powdered chimney bricks and mashed bed-springs.

Now our nice old American ladies are second in spunk and sprightliness to no other old ladies on earth. So maybe they want to wait until the war comes over here, just to be sure that no one is kidding them, to be positive that being bombed or chased by a sixty-ton tank is actually as nerve-racking as the newspapers claim.

In which case, I, who am made of softer stuff, ask them to bridle their curiosity and accept the evidence of the rotogravure sections and the newsreels, and please let's arrange to have wars fought in someone else's backyard instead of ours.

However, if they think by sitting back and waiting until the other side is good and ready to come over here, we can avoid war, I suggest that they confer with the nice old ladies of Poland, Finland, Norway, Denmark, Belgium, Holland, Luxemburg, France, Monaco and Roumania. The soldiers of these ten countries did not go marauding abroad to fight on foreign soil. They waited until the enemy was good and ready to give them the works, let him pick his own time to fight on their soil rather than on his, with results that the old ladies of those countries presently saw without double lens spectacles and heard without benefit or need of ear trumpets.

So instead of an international youth congress, I would propose the convocation of an International Age Congress where our nice old ladies could meet with those of Poland, Finland, Norway, Denmark, Belgium, Holland, Luxemburg, France,

Monaco and Rumania, and exchange thoughts with them on just how bright it is to fight a war on your own country's soil.

But let us now turn to youth—and American youth seems to be very realistic. Shortly after I returned from seven months in Europe, I encountered a tall, blond, tweedy and realistic specimen on a Long Island week-end. The subject had come up of just what we would do if the Japanese should occupy the Dutch East Indies, and someone had suggested that maybe we should oppose this if we were able to. The languid realist who was draping himself over the modernistic furniture of the terrace, drawled:

"Have you ever compared the cost of defending the Dutch East Indies with what it would cost us to erect our own artificial rubber plants?"

No one had, and all of them were concerned as to what would happen to our trade with South America if the Nazis moved in. On this subject he was even more realistic.

"If they are as good as that, wouldn't it be smart to join them rather than to oppose them?" he argued. "After all, if they are going to run the world, it would be to our interest to get a seat at the council table."

"And what makes you think we could get one?"

"Why, don't be silly! It is quite as much to their interest as it is to ours. Of course we could get a very good one."

"In other words, we should just be very realistic about it?"

"After all, why not?"

"Maybe you would like to know what the Nazis think of that type of realism. After all, they have a few realists in their ranks."

"Obviously."

"They would narrow their eyes, and smile, and say nothing—

to you—and among themselves they would point out that, because the Western democracies are so corrupted with your type of short-sighted, greedy, Jewish materialism, they are always easy to beat."

"But obviously I'm not a Jew."

"Of course not. And neither are most Jews, in that sense. I am simply falling into the Nazi lingo. They are sure that the Western democracies are so fat and flaccid in their thinking that they make the mistake of believing anyone can be bought off at a sufficient price. If they know you are willing to buy them off with concessions in Austria, or in Czechoslovakia, or in South America, always weighing the cost of your financial losses against the cost of a war, they will do business on that basis so long as it suits them.

"In other words, they let you buy them off, step by step, as long as you have any money left. When you haven't, or when you decide you don't want to sell any more, then they come in and take over."

It occurs to me that there is a deeper realism in this Nazi attitude than in the policy of continually paying increasing amounts of blackmail to avoid a war.

The trouble with our American realists is that they are up against a crazy kind of idealism. Their biggest mistake is in the assumption that the National Socialists do not mean what they say. This Nazi creed is simple. It runs to the effect that the Aryan German was designed by destiny to rule the world. And the error our American "realists" make is in attempting to see this in economic terms, in assuming that presently it can be placated or bought off. There have been many great movements in history which were not economic, and this is one of them. After all, the Mohammedans did not start out in the year 800 to conquer the known world for the purpose of benefiting the fat merchants in their bazaars.

The Nazis have studied, thoroughly understand and deliberately encourage this type of American realism, so everybody who starts out to give this country bad advice (this includes the German short wave propaganda) leads off by saying that America should be realistic. It happens that Mr. Chamberlain was realistic before us. He was realistic about the Russian alliance, and about all of England's friends in Europe. He realistically allowed the Nazis to butcher the Czechs—and the munitions plants at Skoda made many of the tanks which have since overrun Europe. He was realistic about the Spanish Loyalists, turning them over to the Russians while the Fascists throttled them, with the result that Italy and Germany were in a position to pick off Gibraltar any time they needed it. He was realistic about Poland, so there was no Allied attack while Germany conquered the Poles. He was realistic about Norway, keeping his main forces at home for fear the German assault on Norway might be a mere feint—with the result that Nazi planes could use Stavanger to bomb Scotland.

The particular kind of two-bit, astigmatic realism which England practiced in the 1930's brought her to the brink of disaster. So I suggest that we get sentimental, and stand by our friends while we have a few left, and I'll bet you Tiny Tim's crutch against a machine gun that the pay-off will be bigger in the end. And in this connection, I remember the viewpoint expressed last year to me by one of the smartest American correspondents in Berlin, who knew the Nazis better than any living American.

"I am not afraid about our country," he said, "from the military standpoint. There is the Atlantic Ocean. There is also the fact that potentially we are the greatest military power in the world. We can take anything they can dish up in the way of shot and shell. But I wonder if we can stand up to their woo."

"They are not flinging much of it now."

"They will, though," he said, "and they are experts at it. It's got them where they are today. They take them one at a time."

"With the aid of a few mechanized divisions?"

"Mostly the woo," he said, "more than you'd think. For instance, when they went into Austria they flung woo at everybody, insisted they had absolutely no more territorial demands in Europe. Remember?"

"Who doesn't?"

"Quite a few forgot it temporarily. Then just before they walked into the Sudeten, they turned all their woo on the Poles, concentrated it into a very fine, hard stream. They had this ten-year treaty of friendship and non-aggression with the Poles—"

"How many years has that got to run?"

"About five more," he said. "Anyway the Nazis then insisted that the Poles were their only true pals, that Beck was the one ruler in Europe Hitler could really deal with—their great allies against the Reds. So Beck stood aside while the Nazis gobbled up the Czechs. Even whittled off a piece for himself."

"Then what about the woo?"

"As soon as they had what they wanted, they turned it on the Russians. Signed a non-aggression treaty with them so they could clean up the Poles—and the French—and the British."

"Then if they should get away with it, will they come after us?"

"Not immediately. They will go right through the Balkans into the Ukraine to bite off a big piece of Russia."

"And who will get the woo?"

"We will get it, and it will be very, very good. And I hope we will be smarter than the Poles and the Russians. They will insist that they have absolutely no aspirations outside Europe, so why should we bother with conscription or taxes for a big navy? They will waft the woo at us gently, in big, sticky double-handfuls. It will look very plausible—and popular, too, because peace and low taxes are always popular in any country—only the minute the Nazis have cleaned up on Russia they will grab for South America—say in 1941 or 1942."

"But meanwhile we will be getting the woo?"

"That and offers of a gilt-edged, morocco-bound, hundred-year treaty of non-aggression and brotherly love, guaranteeing the Monroe Doctrine, anything to keep us quiet—until they are ready," said the man who knows the Nazis best of all.

I spent more than half the year in Europe learning just one important thing, namely and to wit: That democracy is not a substitute for determination and brains. These are what the European democracies lacked—and there they are. If we are to survive (and we are going to) we must quit being as stupid and as greedily soft as they were.

So now let us get right down to recent cases. Every time there has been a European crisis during the past five years, the American labor organizations have passed resolutions condemning Nazis and the Fascists as nasty aggressors. Of course it cost nothing to draft and unanimously adopt them. But when we started to get this country in shape to defend itself with an adequate body of trained soldiers, both Mr. Lewis and Mr. Green came out firmly against conscription when it was first proposed. So those pious resolutions which labor passed against the Nazis turn out to be worth exactly a dime a dozen. They were for opposing Fascism provided that nobody was inconvenienced by the effort, and so long as it could be done with a mimeograph.

And now let us turn to look at capital, whose spokesmen have been snorting around against totalitarian restrictions on trade and who, from time to time, were denouncing Roosevelt as a dictator. Were the Chambers of Commerce for preparedness? Yes—provided, however, that some kind of a government tank factory was established in every cross-roads hamlet; provided that the new American war industries are not located by industrialists and soldiers, with an eye to their safety from bombardment, their efficiency of operation or the availability of power or raw material in the neighborhood. Instead, they wanted the war industries parcelled out by politicians like a pork barrel rivers and harbors bill, to make sure that every little hog got all four feet in the armament trough. To this end during the campaign they bothered both Roosevelt and Willkie, with some success, and they have been blackmailing their congressmen, governors and senators, trying to spread the impression that any statesman who fails to bring back from Washington at least one hand-grenade factory for his district is probably a fifth columnist and thereby merits defeat.

The only group which apparently does not want to make a profit out of our defense preparations and instead is ready to endure considerable sacrifice for them, is about a hundred million plain, ordinary citizens who deeply dislike Fascism and intend to go to any length to keep it out of this country. The families of the boys who will have to go to war do not expect or want to profit by it. They don't need to be bribed to be patriotic by being guaranteed a new machine-gun factory or by the assurance that their present scale of profits or standard of hours and wages will not be cut. The rank and file of the American workers are distinguished from some of their more vociferous leaders by a quiet acceptance of responsibility in their country's defense.

The plain people of this country have in them the same stuff that it took to endure that Valley Forge winter or to win the Battle of Antietam. But you would never have guessed it when you listened to the yammering of the cash and carry patriots.

But reverting for a moment to youth: The majority are not flabby or commercially minded. But some of the best of them, particularly those who can think independently, are still confused and somewhat paralyzed, due to the fact that their thinking was deeply permeated with Stalinist notions and guided by Stalinist leaders. It is normal and healthy for youth to be in revolt and to look out to far horizons. This tendency was very thoroughly organized and exploited by the Stalinists in the early and middle thirties, with great success until the coming of the Russo-German pact. Now it happens that Russia in this period had an excellent foreign policy. I happen to be one of those who admired the Russian foreign policy until August, 1939, not because it was Russian but because it was good. When Stalin, in 1939, for reasons which depended entirely on Russian geographical and military situations, saw fit to reverse it, I saw no reason why I should continue to follow it simply because it was a Russian foreign policy. After all, I am an American. The Russian foreign policy is probably excellent from the purely Russian point of view. Events since the beginning of the European war have disclosed that Russia is incapable of fighting a major offensive war against a first-class power, and this, in itself, was a sufficient justification for the pact with Hitler—from a purely Russian standpoint.

My argument to American Youth is that we are not Russians, and there is no reason why this should influence us. If it was wise at the time of the Spanish Civil War and the Munich crisis for the free, democratic powers to oppose totalitarian aggression,

I think the arguments are even stronger today. I fail to see how any American can make that fine Stalinist distinction between the war in the East and the war in the West. Obviously, Stalin was unable to oppose Hitler and therefore had to make the best deal that he could, in order to avoid armed conflict, leaving him free to deal with Japan in the East. But I think it is nonsense for Americans to babble that what goes on in Europe can be no concern of ours, and at the same time screech for aid to the Chinese, although I happen to be in favor of it. Stalin is conducting a realistic foreign policy, based on Russia's actual position in the world balance of power. But our geographical and economic position in the world is necessarily different. I see no reason why any American should confuse the two.

2

THE FOREIGN OFFICE and the Propaganda Ministerium in Berlin are staffed with specialists on American democracy, just as our Department of Agriculture in Washington contains trained experts on the habits and life cycle of the Japanese beetle. The ultimate purpose of both bureaus is the same. The Berlin American experts are very well informed in our manners, customs, and political habits. Of course not all of them hate America. Hate is an emotion which can interfere with scientific skill. You may be sure that some of our Department of Agriculture experts admire the copper-bronze markings of the individual Japanese beetle.

The Berlin experts know their job well. They would have explained to you last winter that they were perfectly aware of the fact that Americans sympathize with the Allies. This was understandable because America is a democracy. Even without this fact, they recognized that our foreign policy has, during most of our term of separate national existence, leaned heavily on the fact that a friendly Britain possessed the world's largest fleet.

"We know," the Nazis would explain, "that American opinion is not only against us but that this feeling in America is growing. It is our business to chart and to predict the rapidity of this rate of growth. We think it probable that by 1942 a majority of American opinion will be ready to enter the war."

"But"—and here you would get a gentle smile—"this war will be over in 1940."

To date the Nazi strategists have made few important mistakes. A minor error was that, after the Russian alliance, the foreign office really did not think that war would follow their invasion of Poland. However, they were prepared for war should it occur. All during the fall of 1939 they rather expected that the Allies would accept peace. But by January of 1940 they were already preparing their people for the fact that the war could only be ended by a quick German offensive which, as I then was able to write, would come around one or the other flanks of the Maginot Line, probably through Holland. In January, 1940, the German people were being told that their victorious armies would be back home by August. But it was also clear that, even if the war was not settled by that time, German morale was sufficiently strong to carry on considerably beyond it.

In the course of his duties, an American correspondent in Berlin does a certain amount of official luncheoning with Nazi officials who are detailed to ride herd on the foreign press. One such American expert has hanging in his office an ancient colored map of the original thirteen colonies.

"This is to remind you," he explains jovially, "that America was also once a small country."

Most of these Nazi experts on America were once exchange students in our Universities. They went to Harvard or Columbia or the University of Kansas and while there often became Betas or Phi Gams, so there you are, in Berlin, with your old college chums. Always with the difference that you are also a Japanese beetle. They will explain to you that they know America well because, in process of working on a Harvard Ph.D. on "German Agriculturalist Minorities in America," they have toured the small towns of the Middle West, perhaps also acting as circulation agents for German-language papers the purpose of which was to keep alive among "our people" in America a consciousness of their German cultural heritage.

In the official luncheons which you must eat with them, both sides strive to guide the conversation away from dangerous topics, and to keep it on perfunctory subjects, because each of you recognize the dangerous gulf in viewpoint. And the luncheons are assumed by both sides to be an unpleasant but important chore.

I well remember my first. We sat down at a pleasant table in a quiet club. The food was excellent because many of the club members were Prussian junkers who brought in from their landed estates game and fowl, which are unrationed, but which are almost unprocurable by the German housewife in the ordinary markets, and are rare even in the better hotels. I remember I lunched on a splendid medallion of broiled goose liver as big as my fist.

"From what part of America do you come?" inquired my host pleasantly.

I answered that I came from the Middle West. He said that he had travelled extensively there and knew it well. Now we both were searching for things to say which were pleasant, and also true, so I said, "We have in the Middle West many fine Americans of German origin, and we are very glad to have them. There are no better people. They make splendid American citizens."

Then I could see that I had startled, perhaps mildly offended him. Yet quickly he got control of his face.

"Yes, yes," he said, "I think perhaps that is true. I know your region well, and have made a particular study about people who live there. Most of them came following the Revolution of 1848. They were mere peasants or workers. Ignorant people of no true culture whatever. Naturally such people, having no culture of their own, would easily pick up whatever culture they came in contact with. So I think you can accurately say, Mr. White, that in this case they do make good American citizens. Yes, I am certain that would be true."

It is interesting to find this racial-cultural analysis applied to a substantial section of the American people. I offer it to Mr. Wendell Willkie, for in spite of the fact that last summer we nominated for the Presidency one of these democratic Americans of German origin, I wonder if he realizes that he comes from "an oppressed German minority which is denied its real rights!" I have this on the authority of the Chicago Bund. You may be sure that the Bund which is directly but invisibly controlled by Berlin just as closely as is the German Consulate, is not given to loose utterances unless they serve the official purpose of the National Socialist Party. This German minority, the Chicago Bund leader explained, is grievously discriminated against, denied its true rights, oppressed and persecuted.

The words could be a direct quotation from former leaders of Austrian, Czech or Polish National Socialist leaders. The technique followed by the carefully organized propaganda in Central Europe may presently have more than an academic interest for America.

All populations of Central Europe are mixed. In Poland there has been, since the beginning of history, a German-language minority, one among many others. For centuries this German minority lived at peace with its Polish neighbors. When the National Socialist agitation first come into Poland many of the more clear-headed German-speaking Poles were alarmed and angry. Their relations with their neighbors had been pleasant. They saw nothing but trouble in the new movement which was reaching out to the young. Yet the dilemma of all German-speaking peoples in Central Europe was and is this:

If they joined the movement and it was unsuccessful, they would suffer no serious after-effects from the easygoing tolerant majorities in the countries where they lived. However, if they did not join it, and it was successful, bitter vengeance would be unleashed on them by the victorious Nazis. They would be branded as traitors to the German race.

Consequently the more timorous of them began to pay lip service to the movement as a form of insurance. They would say privately,

"Of course I don't believe in this, yet it may be safer to be seen at a meeting once in a while, or to have my name inscribed on the official rolls."

When such a German-speaking Pole appeared at his first meeting, however, he would be amazed to find hundreds of apparently sensible compatriots carefully applauding at the proper pauses in the oratory. He would begin to think that perhaps he was mistaken. Perhaps all German-speaking Poles were unanimous for National Socialism. Presently in his bewilderment he would be swept along by the movement.

The thinking of all Central Europe today is in deep confusion. And an American travelling there is constantly beset by a single question. Poles and Hungarians and Yugoslavs and Czechs will say to you almost fearfully, "Now in America, where all European races are treated alike, where you have no discriminatory laws and where all Europeans have equal chances, it isn't true, is it, that Germans are superior?"

"Germans are very good people," you answer, "but I wouldn't say that they are markedly superior to any other race."

All Central Europe looks to America as the great laboratory test tube. If all Germans as such were endowed with the mythical superiority claimed for them by the Nazis, in a free country like America they would immediately rise as a mass to positions of dominance over people of English or Polish or Irish or Bohemian or Scotch origin. Constantly the non-Germans of Central Europe want to be reassured that in America this is not true, that Germans possess no monopoly of all racial virtues.

To understand public opinion in Europe today, you must never lose sight of two facts: The first one is that nothing succeeds like success. As Hitler points out, histories are usually written by the victors; a military success can completely alter a point of view. The second fact you must remember is that organized propaganda can paralyze thought processes. In the older generation, which has learned to make up its own mind, propaganda simply starves them by depriving them of all but one set of available facts. The new generation, however, which has developed under the spell of propaganda, never acquires the ability to discriminate between facts, and I have in mind the young man whom I met on the train as I was entering Germany a few months after the war's outbreak.

He was a very pleasant young German. I doubt that he was a party member. I sat next to him in the railway dining car and, seeing that I was an American, he very politely helped me with the menu and with my food cards, which were new to me. After coffee, we talked. He explained that he had acquired his excellent English in the States, which he liked very much. He had been there as a representative of a chemical firm and said many pleasant things about America. He admired very much our technical achievements in the field of chemistry, a subject of which, of course, I knew nothing. There were many other things about us that he liked. Finally he said:

"But frankly, there is something about America which I did not understand. It was your newspapers."

"Oh, of course," I said, "they were probably too sensational."

"Not at all that," he said. "I thought that technically they were excellent. The first time I saw an American newspaper I marvelled at the comprehensiveness of its news from all over the world. Your newspaper pictures are far better than the ones in German newspapers. Then I turned to the editorial page and read the leading article. It was logical, orderly and concise. It marshalled its arguments with great clarity and moved easily to a logical conclusion. But the next day I picked up another newspaper. I turn to its editorial page and"—you could see the confusion on his face—"it said just the opposite!

"So I feel," he said gently and firmly, "that it is much better in Germany where the government takes the precaution of determining which facts are correct, and giving the people only the truth. Then there is no danger that the people will become confused."

Now, of course, in Germany there were and probably still are a few confused people. It is very easy for an American to underestimate the deep and almost religious zeal of the National Socialist party. It is, but yet it is not, a racket. It has starved the German people and deprived them of many pleasant things. Americans forget the rewards that it promises, which are as extravagant as the sacrifices it demands. The doctrine of the dominant German Aryan and the dominant German Aryan's proper place in the world, which will presently be attained by force of arms, is more glamorous to the German people than we know, and is confidently held before their eyes by the German press.

I entered Germany disagreeing with the Nazis on most doctrinal points but they sold me on one, for I left the country sharing their contempt for German liberals if the breed is judged by specimens now at liberty within the Reich, fluttering around, talking in strained hisses behind their hands. The exceptions to this rule are those with sufficient courage to get themselves into concentration camps. At least they were willing to try to do something about it instead of whispering to each other and feeling sorry for themselves. It is true that you find the fragile flower of liberalism blooming even within the supposedly solid ranks of the Nazi party, and the position of these malcontents is something like this: On days when things seem to be going particularly good for Hitler at home or abroad, they are not noticeably liberal and seem completely resigned to the fate of becoming members of a world-ruling caste with the right to push Slavs off the sidewalks of Central Europe and to lord it over the Dutch, the Belgians and the French. But whenever things momentarily look dark for the Third Reich, then their secret liberalism comes peeping out. They explain in detail why they had to join the party in order to keep their businesses going or to hold their jobs. They begin mourning the loss of their liberties, and yearning for the brotherhood of man. Hitler can have them.

Since I am not a Nazi, I don't subscribe to the doctrines that there are basic psychological differences between the races of mankind, except, perhaps, individual differences in the capacity to acquire and use knowledge, which can be only very roughly determined by differences of size in the human cranium. But environmental pressures, acting on the European Germans, have produced great psychological differences there.

The European Germans are a people of many talents—for cleanliness, for thrift, for science, for precision in mechanical instruments—but their talent for self-pity is monumental.

So they are at the mercy of any demagogue who will expertly massage their tear glands and get them to blubbering in unison about their own wrongs, which are the Treaty of Versailles, or the climate, or the fact that they are discriminated against, or that they lack colonies, or the fact that there are too many Germans. The remedy for this overcrowding is to produce more Germans, so that there will be enough Germans to take land away from other people, so that there will be facilities for producing more Germans and overcrowding it.

Now the Swedes once lost a big war and a lot of territory. But because they lack the German talent for self-pity they shut up, went to work and produced a clean, neat industrious country whose standard of living is a model for all Europe. If they had had the German genius for snivelling over their wrongs, they would have starved themselves (snivelling the while) to produce a gigantic armament with which to bother everybody else.

Yet the Germans last winter were far from enthusiastic about the war. I used to watch them as they gathered at five o'clock tea-time in the Hotel Bristol in Berlin, while the string orchestra was playing in the thickly carpeted grand salon. All the tables were full and at many of them were young German officers and their girls, or perhaps they were with their parents and their sisters. The boys, by their faces, might have been Dartmouth or Yale seniors.

For the most part they were young lieutenants, a little uncertain in their new finery, and their scrubbed, pink faces were stiff and sober. Most of them were on week-end leave from the West Wall. Their girls, all of whom were wearing dowdy German hats, would try to ease things with their gay chatter, but Germans have little gift for small talk. I remember one family group, the old father—his red cheeks laced with duelling scars, close-cropped white hair, wing collar and in sober Sunday black; the dowdy, plump mother, a sister and a couple of younger brothers, also pink, combed, scrubbed and in black, who couldn't take their eyes off the young lieutenant's gleaming silver epaulets. At this table they are all having tea and now the pastry wagon rolls by them over the thick carpet.

With a gesture the proud old father halts it: A gorgeous array of cakes and pastries, meringues, white, pink and chocolate icings, cream and custard fillings—rare then in Germany but still in costly abundance at hotels like the Bristol. For the young lieutenant who must go back to the West Wall, a huge piece of cake with chocolate icing. The old man insists he must take it. For the two younger brothers, whose eyes glitter at the tray, a single eclair, to be divided between them. For the mother, the sister, the old father, nothing. Maybe they aren't hungry. But they proudly watch the young lieutenant eat.

The music stops and there is a sudden hush in the undertone of talk as the big radio loudspeaker is switched on. The very, very confident voice of the Nazi announcer first gives news of an air dog-fight over England—of course a German victory—and Germany now has absolute control of the North Sea. Then away from the news and the confident account of the power and the spirit of ninety million German people.

These prosperous, upper-class people listen gravely and anxiously to the clear, confident Nazi voice. But their faces do not light up when he talks of German victories. There was little confidence in Berlin, under the brooding shadow of the West Wall, although the news announcers were confident and the string orchestra plucked out pretty little tunes and the girls and wives of the officers did their best to break up those long silences.

Of course, the sweeping victories of the spring and summer have greatly changed this. But it is certainly true that only a dictatorship could have forced them into a war for the dominance of Europe. Such a program could never have commanded a majority in a democratic Germany, although there can be no doubt that a majority is now jubilant over its results. This you can be certain of, in spite of the censorship which, because of German victories, has tightened rather than relaxed. Last winter the censorship on outgoing dispatches to America was very liberal, for the reason that the Nazis then felt a need to conciliate American opinion, which they do not regard as pressing today.

I went into the matter of censorship as soon as I arrived in Berlin, and was assured by a veteran correspondent that the foreign press was left fairly free by the Nazis.

"And that is smart of them," he explained. "They know public opinion back in the States is strong against them. They know it wouldn't stand for a white-wash job and any newspaperman who tried to put one over would be called home, so there isn't much censorship."

"Outside of military stuff?"

"Of course. Beyond that just a few simple rules."

"Such as?"

"Well, don't ever say anything nasty in a personal way about the Boy Himself. They don't like that at all. Very sensitive about him. That would get you thrown out quick."

"Even though their newspapers are free to refer to Roosevelt as a Jewish dwarf?"

"Even though."

"But anything else goes?"

"Not quite. Whenever you get hold of something they won't like, be doubly sure of your facts. They will usually take it if you make it stick. Of course, if you are consistently nasty to them over a long period of time, they may give you up and send you over the border. It is better to keep your stuff balanced."

"Balanced?"

"Whenever you get hold of something hot, try to include in the same story something pleasant which is also true, for instance, a note that nobody here is undernourished and that most of them are strong for the regime. And I would be careful about adjectives."

"Not use any?"

"Use temperate ones. For instance, instead of writing that 'the Nazi policy of Jew persecution is now being extended to Bohemia with that savage brutality to which Germans have long been calloused,' I think I would say instead that 'the policy of new Germany toward Jewish minorities is being extended to Bohemia with that unflagging zeal and unswerving determination which characterizes National Socialism.' They like that better and the facts are the same in both cases. They aren't ashamed of their Jewish policies. If you use the wrong adjectives they are liable to come and reason with you."

"At night, with rubber hoses?"

"Oh, never. You are an American. Very polite and agreeable young officials who speak better English than you do and reason with you in the most pleasant and gentlemanly way."

For ten days I spoke from Berlin over short wave radio to America. I had to prepare in advance four typewritten copies of each talk. These I would fold into the vest pocket of my trench coat and carry with me to the big German short-wave studios out in Adolph Hitler Platz on the outskirts of Berlin. This, like all radio studios in Europe, was carefully guarded. A radio station in modern warfare is an important military objective both in war and in civil disturbances.

Arriving at the studios an hour before the broadcast, I would present my pass to the steel-helmeted S.S. guards at the entrance. And in the course of the evening at least half a dozen such guards would demand to see it. Arriving at the censorship office in the top of the building, I would deliver my four manuscript copies. One of them went to the military censor, another went to the political censor, a third I was allowed to keep myself to read over the microphone, and a fourth went to the official who conducted me to the broadcasting booth and who followed it with his eyes as I read from my copy, to make sure that I made no changes from the text after it had been approved. If I would have attempted an alteration, he would have thrown a switch and cut me off the air.

The military censor was easy. Any correspondent knows that it is improper to attempt to send out news of troop movements. Occasionally, however, there was something to learn. I did not realize, for instance, when I arrived in Berlin that all mention of the weather is taboo, in any warring country.

You could not say for instance, "Tonight is clear, cold and crisp with a star-spangled sky over the Berlin blackout," first because it is corny, and second because announcement of the fact that there are no clouds constitutes an invitation for enemy bombers to shellack the place.

The political censor, however, was more difficult. Sitting in the adjoining room waiting for him to finish with my dispatch, I frequently would hear him pick up the telephone, call the foreign office or the Propaganda Ministerium, and read into the receiver a rapid-fire Geman translation of what I had just written in English.

One afternoon the American correspondents in Berlin were invited by the Propaganda Ministerium to a special preview of a movie. The Nazi propaganda machine controls not only the radio and the newspapers but the movie theaters as well. The newsreel company is only a branch of the state propaganda machine. This particular offering was the official German newsreel which was to be released in all German theaters the following Monday. Most of it was a series of shots of the German advance into Poland which had just been edited and released. But the preview also included a few feet from an American newsreel, which in some way had found its way to Berlin.

This was unusual, for German newsreels usually pay little attention to what happens outside the Reich. The American section of the film still contained its subtitles in English, which of course would be removed before the picture was shown to the German people. These English subtitles explained that the film was a competition in hat designing conducted by the girls of a California high school.

American millinery styles in the fall of 1939 were definitely cockeyed. An American audience would have gotten a smile out of the shots of these little girls parading in their fantastic creations. But the Nazi propaganda machine never includes anything just because it would give German audiences a few minutes of mild amusement. There always must be a definite propaganda reason. This reason I did not clearly understand until I heard from the sound track the voice of the German announcer which had been dubbed into this American film.

"German women!" roared the strident voice, "Here we see how the Jews are trying to insult, degrade and make ridiculous the women of America with these fantastic styles. Thank God such things are not permitted under the Third Reich!"

Yet for half a minute even this was not quite clear, until the American correspondent sitting next to me, with a nudge and a whisper, reminded me that the morning papers had carried the announcement of the new clothing rationing scheme, under the terms of which German women would have to wear last year's coat and hat for the duration of the war, and would be allowed to purchase only about four pairs of cotton stockings and one dress per year. Then you could see why the theory that all new styles were a Jewish plot to insult womanhood, was of definite propaganda value to the Nazis.

It occurred to me that this little incident might fit into a broadcast. That night in a very few words at the end I chronicled the fact that in the afternoon I had attended an advance showing of a Nazi newsreel which showed a California high school style competition which the German sound track announcer said was an example of how Jews were attempting to make American women ridiculous. I quoted the exact words of the sound track announcer without comment. But that night the Nazi censor in the short wave radio building shook his head firmly.

"No, Mr. White," he said. "We cannot permit you to say that over the radio to America."

"But I am only giving what I saw in the newsreel I was invited to see by your Propaganda Ministerium. I am sure that I quote it correctly."

"There is no doubt of that," he said. "It happens I myself this afternoon attended the preview you refer to. You have correctly quoted the incident, but we cannot permit you to say it over the air, for the reason that it might create in America, anti-German feeling."

There you see the technique. They want to do it to us, but they do not want us to know that they are doing it.

Shortly after that *Der Stürmer* carried a lengthy article proving that Winston Churchill was a Jew. I put this into a broadcast, and included also the comment that the Nazis had drilled into the German people a bitter hatred of Jews and that, whenever a propaganda barrage was turned on a nation, such charges were always included.

I recalled the fact that several weeks previously, when America had been heavily under fire in the German press, *Der Stürmer* had charged that Roosevelt was a Jew, offering as proof the fact that the President's mother's name was Sarah. Again I had difficulty with the censor. Again he did not question the facts, which were above reproach since the Nazi press frequently refers to Roosevelt as a "Jewish dwarf." But again he brought up the argument that such facts would create in America feeling against the Nazis.

3

THE GERMAN PEOPLE have learned their propaganda lesson well. Nothing that happened to me in Germany became that country so well as my leaving of it—from the little Prussian port of Sassnitz, where I was to take the steamer for Sweden en route to cover the Finnish war which had just broken out. Incidentally, the German people had not yet learned that this war was in progress, although it was making top headlines in every newspaper in the free world. The German propaganda machine had not yet decided what line to take. Since their control over the press and radio is absolute, they have ample leisure in which to make up their minds, since they need not contradict or explain any news story which they do not permit to be published.

Before I left Berlin, I asked if I might take pictures en route to Sweden.

"But of course you can take pictures in Germany," the bright young attaché in the Propaganda Ministerium had insisted. "Naturally not at the West Wall or of fortifications, but of anything else."

Yet Berlin turned out to be a very sophisticated and urbane place, although I did not realize it at the time.

Now I happen to know small towns, so I was particularly interested in Sassnitz. It is a little northern village where the sun barely gets above the horizon in winter and then comes palely through chill fog. The occupations of Sassnitz are fishing for herring and patriotism. Although in Berlin I had become used to seeing Hitler's picture in shop windows, I did not know what German patriotism was until I came to Sassnitz. Der Fuehrer scowled out of the druggist's window, among the display of pharmaceuticals. He scowled out of the baker's window. He scowled from the window of a store which had gone out of business, but the owner of the location had built a patriotic window display around the scowl, pending a new tenant.

The people of Sassnitz are very blond, with thick necks. The women have stringy hair which they wash constantly with laundry soap, they are all a deathly pale because there is little sun, and they patriotically scowl back at the patriotic window displays, and then scowl patriotically at one another to make sure that everyone else is scowling patriotically.

In the leading department store's central window was a patriotic display provided, according to the explanatory card, by the Ladies' Auxiliary of the National Socialist Party. In the center was an almost life-size portrait of der Fuehrer, scowling out at you from an evergreen wreath patriotically woven by the scowling women of Sassnitz. Underneath was a placard which began: "How would you like this, German women?" Then followed the text which explained that one of the British war aims is to divide Germany, and then import black men into Prussia for the purpose of polluting the racial blood purity of the women of Sassnitz. All the scowling little children read this sign, and the scowling men and women of Sassnitz. Then they look up at der Fuehrer's picture, whose scowl reassures them that this shall never happen to the scowling women of Sassnitz.

After photographing this, and also a parade of scowling steel-helmeted soldiers down the main street, I went to the principal restaurant of the village for lunch. As I opened the door all the men sitting at the tables, drinking beer, looked up, scowled, raised their right hands and said: "Heil Hitler!"

"Guten Tag!" I answered, and smiled, which a foreigner must always do in Germany, particularly when he does not return the salute, which no self-respecting foreigner ever does. Then I turned to the barman and asked if he could tell me when the steamer left for Sweden, and please to speak slowly, because I was an American.

Before he could answer, the man with the thick, red neck, near the door, who had shouted "Heil Hitler!" the loudest, mumbled: "We could tell you were some kind of a damned foreigner because you did not return the salute."

I smiled pleasantly as though I had not understood, or realized that what he said was directed to me. This is also sometimes a useful thing to do in Germany. All the other men laughed. The barman smiled, too, but he did tell me when the steamer left for Sweden.

So then I sat down and asked for a menu. The barman's wife scowled and said: "We have only herring." I said I would have herring. As I ate, I noticed that a couple of teen-age kids in the uniform of the Hitler Jugend, which is a very patriotic organization for children, were scowling and leering at me through the window. Then I remembered that I had noticed this same pair several times that morning while I was taking pictures on the main street. Children in small towns often follow foreigners around, but these were a little too old for that. If they had been following me ever since I had snapped the parade, they must have been lurking behind me for several hours. But why were they waiting and grinning outside now as I ate my herring? And at this point a hand fell on my shoulder, just as hands fall on shoulders in detective stories, and I turned to look up at a sergeant and two soldiers in steel helmets, standing stiffly at attention.

"Come with me," said the sergeant. "You are under arrest."

The sergeant led me into the guardroom. The two soldiers in steel helmets marched behind us. The guardroom was small and filled with cigar smoke. There was one window.

"Why did you not register with the police when you came to Sassnitz?"

"Because I only got in last night. I signed the hotel register. Today I take the steamer for Sweden."

"You say you are an American. Have you a passport?"

I pulled it out.

"Where were you born?"

"In America." I pointed to the line on my passport.

"You say you were born in America. You are sure you are not English?"

I said I was sure.

"You say you are not English. When were you born?"

I told him.

"You say you were born in 1900. How long have you been in Germany?"

"I have been in Germany a month, as your Propaganda Ministerium in Berlin will tell you if you telephone them. Is there anyone here who speaks English? My German is not good."

"It is good enough. Why did you not register with the police?"

"Because I have not been in Sassnitz twenty-four hours. I am only waiting for the boat to Sweden."

"Why do you go to Sweden?"

"Because I am a journalist and am on my way to Finland."

"What will you do in Finland?"

"Write for American newspapers."

"What will you write?"

"What I see there."

"What else will you do?"

"Nothing else."

"You say you are an American. Then you like the Finns very much—no?"

I said I could not tell, I had never been in Finland.

"Maybe you like Finns better than you like Germans—no?"

I said I had never known a Finn, and so could not answer this.

"America will come into the war—no?"

I said that, when I left America, I thought America would not come into the war.

The sergeant smiled.

"Then America will not come in. Instead, America will—[here he held out one hand, palm upward, thick fingers slightly curled, and shook it as though jingling imaginary coins]—make much money—no? America will do that, you say?"

I said I had not said America would do that, it was he who had said it. And at this moment the door opened and the lieutenant came in. The lieutenant was about thirty-five and slim, with a lean face and blue-gray eyes. The sergeant and all the other soldiers in the guardroom stood at attention. The lieutenant looked at me. His face was without expression.

"You may sit down, if you like," he said in English. "You have a camera?"

"Yes."

"Where is it?"

"In my trenchcoat pocket." I pulled it out. "It is a very good camera," I said, "a German camera, the best."

"You have taken pictures with it?"

"Yes. Your Propaganda Ministerium in Berlin told me I could take pictures anywhere in Germany except, of course, of the West Wall or of fortifications. You may telephone them and they will tell you they have said this."

"You have taken pictures here in Sassnitz?"

"Yes."

"What did you take?"

"Many pictures, snapshots in the streets, of store windows, of paintings of der Fuehrer, of school children, of your parade this morning when your soldiers and your band marched down the main street—many pictures."

"Did you take a picture of the railway station—no? It is said you have taken a picture of the railway station."

"Well, I did not," I said. "Why should I want a picture of your station? It is not beautiful."

"No," said the lieutenant, and here he smiled. "The Sassnitz station is certainly not beautiful. But it is also said you have taken pictures of the harbor. Were you down at the harbor this morning?"

"Yes," I said, "and I took a picture. I did not know it was forbidden."

"What was this picture you took?"

"Of that old Swedish square-rigged sailing ship which is anchored there. You can see it from this window."

The lieutenant stepped over and looked at the old Swedish ship.

"You took nothing else?"

"Nothing else."

"Your passport?"

"Your hand is on it."

"Excuse me." He picked it up and spent a minute going through it. "Your permission to leave Germany?"

"Here—and signed by the Police Praesidium in Berlin."

This the lieutenant also read.

"It is all in order," he said. "You may go, but you should not take any more pictures of the harbor, or of the railway station. You understand, of course, that it is because of the war that we must ask you these things."

"Of course I understand. In our last war in America we had to do the same things."

Then I walked out of the guardroom alone, and back to my now stale beer at the bar. The fat Prussians were still sitting at the tables but now they were silent. About half of them wore party buttons. They were whispering when suddenly the door opened and the thick-necked sergeant returned, this time without the two steel-helmeted soldiers. The sergeant was smiling. It was not a nice smile. He walked over to my table and sat down. It should be remembered that I had not asked the sergeant to sit down.

"So you say you go to Finland?" said the sergeant. He spoke no English.

"I am going to Finland," I answered.

"Why?"

"Because of the war there, and because journalists must go many places they do not want to go."

"You told the lieutenant you had been in Berlin a month. How do you like Germany?"

"There is plenty of food here," I said. "Nobody is hungry."

"Maybe you Americans do not like the German people," said the sergeant, and he still had that smile which was not very nice on his face.

"Some of them I like very much," I said. "In America we have many good citizens who were Germans."

"Maybe you don't like our regime?"

"No," I said, "I don't like the regime."

"Why do you say you don't like the regime?"

"Because you asked me," I said. I was getting a little tired of this.

"You told the lieutenant you took pictures this morning of the soldiers in the parade. You find that Germany is very military—no?"

"Yes," I said, "I find that Germany is very military."

"Maybe you Americans don't like this—no?"

"Maybe we don't," I said.

"Maybe it surprises you Americans to see so many German soldiers—no?"

He was still smiling that not very nice smile, even more broadly.

"It doesn't surprise me at all to see German soldiers," I said. "In the past I have seen many more German soldiers than I see in Germany today."

"When was this that you saw so many German soldiers?" asked the sergeant.

"After the last war," I said. "Then I saw a great many German prisoners who had surrendered to our American army."

"But things are different now," said the sergeant. The not very nice smile which I had not liked was not on his face any more.

"Very different now," I said. "The last time I was in Germany, just after the World War, Germans in the Rhineland were much more polite to Americans than they are now." I laid a mark on the table to pay for my beer and stood up.

"Where are you going now?" asked the sergeant.

"To my hotel to write," I said.

"You will write all this for your American papers?"

"If I like."

"You know," the sergeant said, a little uneasily, "that the lieutenant has said your case was clear, and that you could go. You did not need to stay in this room."

"I understood your lieutenant perfectly," I said. "He speaks excellent English and he was polite."

"That is because he has lived in England," said the sergeant proudly.

"Then I can understand it," I said.

"I mean," said the sergeant, "he speaks English so well because he has lived in England."

"I was sure you meant that," I said, and I went on out the door toward my hotel. The two pale and pimply Hitler Jugend kids who had reported me were still there, but they were not leering at me now. They were pretending to be reading the poster put up by the Hitler Ladies' Auxiliary, which explains that the English are planning to import black soldiers into Sassnitz, to pollute Germany's purest Aryan blood.

When I got back to my hotel, I found my landlady in a state of considerable agitation. This was a small town, and of course news traveled fast.

I was going up to my room? she asked anxiously. Yes, to write some articles before the steamer left. But it would be much wiser, she said with a worried look, if I left immediately. Why? The steamer did not leave for two hours. Still, it would be much wiser, she said. I should leave the room immediately, if I did not mind, because who knew, the steamer might leave unexpectedly, sometimes it did. Did I need anybody to help me down with my bags?

I didn't. I paid her and I thanked her and she looked very much relieved as I left the house. I walked down to the pier and sat on my suitcase for an hour looking at the shipping idle in the harbor, and at the big oil tank truck with "Esso" painted in large black letters across its fat white belly, apparently waiting for a tanker which might come over from Sweden or perhaps slip through the British blockade.

When the steamer docked I went through the customs, my German marks were checked, and about ten dollars' worth of them confiscated because I had over the legal limit for a departing traveler, and my baggage was opened and passed by the customs. Then I walked up to the top deck, lit a cigaret, watched the last few travelers straggling up the gangplank, and then turned to the direction of the coast of free Sweden, off beyond the haze. I felt greatly relieved—and at this exact point another of those hands fell on my shoulder and I turned to look at another uniformed Nazi.

"You will please come with me," he said, "and you will bring your bags."

I carried my bags myself, following the Nazi down off the gangplank. There were three of them in the customs room, waiting to give me what was apparently an extra-thorough examination. I was ordered to open the bag. The Nazi inspector took out my suits and my shirts and laid them on the counter.

"What is your occupation?" he said.

"I am a journalist."

"Why should we believe that?"

"It is written on my passport."

"What other proof have you?"

"These letters from my newspaper."

He shuffled through them noncommittally and handed them back.

"Remove the contents of that compartment," he said.

I took out my neckties and laid them on the counter. He bent over the now empty bag and felt in its corners, emerging with a small box.

"What is this?" he said.

"It contains earrings which I bought in Italy."

"Open it," he said, handing it to me.

"You will notice," I said, "that it actually contains earrings and I assure you that I bought them, not for Winston Churchill, but for my wife."

At this point the Nazi official permitted himself a mild smile. "You may go," he said. "Your case is clear. You will pack your bag," and he turned away.

Now every warring country has its spy scares, as America should well remember from our war of 1917. But the Nazis have drilled into the German people a hatred and suspicion of all foreigners which gives their spy scares dramatic overtones.

And then on to Sweden. O wonderful, beautiful, free country! For an hour, long past midnight, on the train to Stockholm from the little seaport town of Alborg, I lay awake after my month in Germany, watching the dazzling beautiful electric bulbs in the street lights of the little free Swedish towns, which flashed by in the night. Delicious little free country where there were no air-raid blackouts—not then, anyway—and where the light bulbs could shine out clear and white as sunshine in the little villages and through the countryside!

Beautiful, free, clean little country where there were no blackouts of the mind, where real news with real headlines and facts stared out at you unafraid from the columns of the papers; where there were books in the bookstores—books which were about something! Where people read and talked and thought as freely as we Americans, and smiled on the streets and said what they liked without fear of spies. Incredibly beautiful Swedish girls—they took your breath away every block—who were free to dress smartly, and to talk lightly, and to smile freely—wonderful girls with smiles as gay and free and innocent as wirehaired puppies—who were not afraid to be glad that they were women, and to wear giddy little hats ("Of course we German women should not dress as you do," a German girl explained to a Swedish one, "for then people might think we German women were not serious.") These marvellous unserious Swedish girls seemed to be as quick-minded and witty as the French, and each so lovely you could pick from any streetcar in Stockholm enough of them to give a Broadway musical show a year's run; girls with skins of cream and hair which is gold vapor, sitting in coffee houses, stuffing their little tummies with such really unbelievable things as cakes, rich and golden yellow with real eggs, frosted high with actual sugar or maybe rich red-brown real chocolate, floating in deep rich pools of genuine whipped cream!

Swell, grand, superb little nation which was preparing—not grimly and with scowls for world conquest—but happily and with smiles for the Christmas season! Where anyone could afford to go up to those magnificent smorgasbord tables and for fifty cents and without meat cards, pile high his plate with big fat sausages from every animal that ever wagged a tail, with sliced smoked venison and orange marmalade, or pickled eels, or spiced or smoked eels, or pickled herring, or smoked or spiced herring, or egg salad, or potato salad, or endive salad, or goose—baked, boiled, roasted or smoked—or turkey the same, or chicken the same, and stuffed with oysters, chestnuts, raisins or all three, and of course with every fish that ever waggled a fin in Sweden's northern seas, and every kind of lobster that ever flapped a flipper in one of Norway's deep fjords and every crab that ever danced on the white sands of Denmark's beaches, boiled or baked or fried, and dripping gold with melted butter!

Gentlemen, stand now and raise your glasses of hot Swedish grog with grated nutmeg quivering on the surface: I give you Sweden—as she was then—skoal!

4

BUT FROM SWEDEN I went on into Finland to find out about war. A great many highly unfavorable things have been written against war. I have written some of them myself, before I ever saw one. Now that I have, I am glad they turned out to be true. Yet there are some nice things about war, only writers are afraid to put them down for fear that some fool may jump to the conclusion that war as a whole is nice, which would be a dangerous and terrible lie. But because I am going to try to give you war as a whole, I will take the risk of telling some of the nice things about it.

Parts of war are like the most interesting hiking or hunting trip you ever took, only war is cleaner and fairer than hunting and is like hunting would be if the quail had automatic rifles and the deer had a 1007 millimeter Bofors gun, and therefore had as good a chance of getting you as you have of killing them. So it is nicer and fairer than hunting, and yet it has the same clean, outdoors feel, the same feel of men all doing something together, the same nice taste of hot coffee and meat and bread after you have worked hard in the open all day, the same nice smell of wood smoke and the same sweet sleep when you are so tired you don't feel that the mattress is straw; the same nice sound of a wood fire crackling at night in the dugout stove after you have hung up both your pairs of wool socks to dry on a string, and laid your boots flat by the stove with their soles almost touching its legs.

But most of all there is the danger, and this, although I am a little ashamed to write it, is the most fun of all, provided, of course, that you do not get killed or hurt, or that no one you know does, or that it doesn't come so often that your nerves go to pieces and you cringe inside a little when you hear one even a long way off.

But leaving all these things out, the danger in being shelled or in dodging a belt-full of machine-gun bullets is like the most exciting moment in the best ball game you ever watched, or like a very tense hand in a bridge game. Because, as in cards, keeping alive in war requires not only plenty of skill but also some luck. For if they deal you the wrong cards (or place the heavy artillery in the right place) then—no matter how skillful you are—you lose the pot, which, in the case of war, is made up not of colored celluloid chips but of arms and legs, some of which may be yours.

Thus we see there is little danger of your getting bored—as I always do at bridge—of losing interest in the game, because it is hard to care who goes set for how many points in diamonds or spades; but if it is arms and legs and they are yours, your mind is always on the game, and you have that same very nice feeling when you come through a tight place and find you have won—only it is very, very, very much nicer.

The night I got to Helsinki, a camera man who had just returned from the northern front was sitting in the center of a group of American reporters in the dining-room, staring at the tablecloth.

"Listen," he said, with one hand gripped tight around a double Scotch, "what gagged you was this silly punk. He had never seen anyone dead before, so all the time he had to be making those jokes of his, to show it didn't bother him. Before it was over I was really hoping the kid would step on a mine, so I wouldn't have to kill him.

"We were at the place where the Finns cut up that Russian brigade, got it wandering around in circles, all tangled up in itself in the woods with the Finns hanging onto its flanks, shooting into the mob as it wandered. What gets you are the ones that almost seem to be standing. You would think they were still alive, like one we almost stumbled over, leaning up against a tree with both hands pressed over his heart where he had got it, only he had been standing there two weeks.

"You see, they froze so fast they didn't have time to die all over like they do in other wars, so their cheeks are still pink and the tops of their ears white from how cold it was then. There was heavy snow in some places, almost up to their waists when it happened, which is the reason some of them seem to be standing. Since then a couple more inches had fallen, and this stuck to them on the side the wind came from, so if you see them from that side they look like snowmen standing out there. I tell you I could have killed that silly punk because it got you the way they looked, and him giggling like a girl and making all those cracks.

"The Russians had had a lot of tanks, and most of these the Finns had managed to get with gasoline grenades. When you would open the tanks and look inside, the men were crisped and shriveled to the size of a twelve-year-old, and all charred black except their teeth, which were very white. How can you write about a thing like that? There were some still alive, because they didn't surrender, and melted off into the woods, and the Finns think they have gone nuts. Because they climb trees and shoot at Finnish burial parties. The Finns can't figure how they have gotten anything to eat, because the battle was more than two weeks ago. The Finns say they hope to get most of them buried in another week, but this will only be those that got mowed down in piles, or that are propped up against something where you can see them, because how can they ever find all the ones who just fell over in the snow and got covered up?

"When along about April it thaws, and the snow melts, then it will be very, very funny up in that country, and I hope they take that punk kid back there and tie him to a tree so he can laugh himself nuts."

However, there are other aspects to war, as I found out on Christmas Eve, and in particular to the little war in Finland. It was, for instance, the most beautiful war that anyone ever saw. Because snow covered everything which is ugly to the eye, such as the wreckage of tanks, while everything that might have been ugly to the nose—and there were numbers of them out there beyond the wire—was frozen solid as marble and covered with snow as well, and so could not be ugly either to the eye or nose until the spring thaw. It was late enough to be dark except that the moon was out as we left the front-line trenches, walking through the spruce forest where many inches of fluffy snow seemed to drip from the branches like great gobs of whipped cream. Along the path it was packed hard. We had our faces to the sound of the guns which was a rising and falling roar. When the ones just back of us were quiet for a minute, you could then hear the ones far away up and down the line.

It was fifty-four degrees below zero, colder than you have ever known. We came into a clearing which let the moonlight down through the snow and here another path intersected with ours and on it we saw four soldiers carrying a very small, light, flat-bottomed boat. There are many lakes in these forests but they had all been frozen deep enough to bear the weight of a thirty-three ton Russian tank for many weeks. One man could easily carry so light a boat, but when they got closer we could see something on top of it and this was not a wounded soldier, it was one who was dead, and we could see how he had died. It could only have been out on the flat lake, because of the position of his arms and legs and head. He could only have died on a very flat surface, face up, and frozen before he was found. His face was very clear in the moonlight and since it was Christmas Eve, I wish I could tell you that his face was still and peaceful. It was still, but it was the face of a man who had died in pain, which is how most soldiers die unless they get it in the head, and never know they get it. But I can at least say this pleasant thing, which is also true, that it is much better to die as he did after a little pain, knowing why you die, than it is to live on for nothing, in fear and slavery, and see your children grow up in this slavery, never knowing that it is slavery.

The soldiers carrying the boat said he had died from a wound low in his side. One of them put an arm out to show us where, and as he did it the button of his sleeve struck against the frozen blood on the man's side, and this clicked as though it were also metal. They said when they found him they knew he was a Finn without looking at his buttons, because, as we could see, his boots had been taken off, since Finnish boots were always much better than the Russians' boots. We asked how long he had been dead, and they said no one could tell, because in this cold a man with even a little wound would freeze, as he was frozen, within an hour, if he had lost much blood, but probably he had died in the morning attack. They said they were bringing all of them in from the lake because the Russians just now were quiet, and because tomorrow would be Christmas. And they said it would not be good to know that Finns were lying out on the lake on Christmas Eve.

So then they went on up the path with their boat.

5

To ROUND OUT an honest picture of war, I should like to include a monograph on the subject of being bombed, jotted down at a time when I had never been bombed until the previous week, and had since then been bombed steadily, and without any regular interruptions for meals. It is compiled for the information of people who have never been bombed, and hope never to be. I can say to them that the worst time of all is just before you are bombed for the first time, and know you are going to be bombed.

This is not fun. First you hear them way off. Then you hear them closer. Then you see them, and also see that they are coming straight at you, and any direction you run in can make no difference at all, because they are coming about two hundred miles an hour, and you cannot know whether to run to the right or left. So you stay where you are, looking up.

Then, just in case you were not already a little scared, the sirens begin a terrific howling, sounding like a covey of banshees being strangled by a herd of gorillas and not liking it at all. Neither do you.

When the actual bombs begin striking the ground, it is not bad. There is only a terrific amount of noise, and you get interested in trying to see the bombs coming down, forgetting that the planes are so high and tiny that you could hardly hope to see anything so small as a bomb until it got very close, and then it would be taveling so fast that you probably could not see it.

Now as for taking cover, your own instincts on that subject are not bad, and these tell you that it is not good to be in buildings which can fall in on you, nor is it good to be out in an open plain where you might get sideswiped by flying steel fragments, but the best place of all is some shallow declivity where, with a casual smile on your face, you can lie down and yet be protected on the sides.

When you have picked your place, you walk to it slowly and with a casual smile on your face, for fear that people who have been bombed often will think you are afraid. But this is only the first time. Because after that, you understand that people who have been bombed before do not give a damn if you are afraid or not, or ever stop to notice that you were casually smiling. So after that you feel free to frown if you like, or to run if you want to, if there is any sense in it, which usually there is not.

The next few times you are bombed are definitely fun. Because you are now certain that you are not afraid, there is no danger that you will make a fool of yourself, and the spectacle of what happens during a bombing—the noise and the howling and the people running like hell—is definitely exciting.

Incidentally, these people who run like hell are usually women who have never been bombed before, or else they are people who have been very close to a bomb which exploded, and maybe helped carry away things under blankets afterward, and so understand from first-hand experience how good the reasons for running like hell sometimes can be.

But after these first few times, being bombed settles down to a routine nuisance, in which you are no longer excited, but hate the noise of the sirens because they mean you probably must leave whatever you are doing, and lunch will be late, and you are also always just a little bit uneasy even when you can hear them dropping way off, and if they begin to drop quite close, you are definitely afraid, which is only sensible.

So you get to hate the sirens when they blow the alarm signal, first because they are scientifically designed to irritate human nerves as much as possible, and then because they mean you must leave what you are doing, and all the rest of it. Also, you hate them again when they blow the all-clear signal, because it means that after all nothing happened to you, and you got interrupted and your day's work disarranged, for no really sensible reason.

So this is what happens when you are bombed, as nearly as I can tell it. It is not nice, but if you think that you would be terribly afraid, you had better go over and get bombed for a while, because you will be relieved to find that you are not.

And now, just a word about the people who fight in wars, starting with those who know why they fight. I remember a night I spent in a front-line dugout on the Mannerheim Line in Finland. To reach it we walked a couple of kilometres through a spruce forest and then into the communication trench for a mile, and then down the front-line trenches for two more miles. They were very quiet, except off to the south we could hear the Russian artillery. The Finns said sometimes they seemed to be shooting at nothing at all. Then we turned off down a communication trench to our dugout, getting into it at midnight. Most of the soldiers were asleep in their bunks but a patrol had just come in which had been out behind the Russian lines on skis, cutting field telephone wires. These men were drying their socks and they had the radio going. A voice was talking in Finnish. When I asked what the station was, the lieutenant explained it was the Moscow radio, that this was the propaganda lecture in Finnish, and that presently the musical hour would begin and the soldiers were waiting for it.

The men were talking with each other, paying no great attention to the propaganda lecture, so I asked the Finnish lieutenant to translate it. He said, speaking along with the loudspeaker voice, that the Finnish soldier should no longer fight the battles of the rich peasants and foreign capitalists, but should kill his officers and desert to the Red army. The lieutenant explained they said about the same thing every night. The leader of the patrol then remarked that just before they had turned back, they had tossed a grenade into the entrance of a Russian dugout. He thought it might be a post-of-command dugout, it was so unusually well built.

Sitting for a minute in the command room, the lieutenant pointed out on a field map just where we were, and the location of our battery and the hill and the lake. I asked again about the men listening to the Russian propaganda talk, telling them to kill their officers, but the lieutenant could see nothing strange in this. He said they all knew why they were fighting, and the Russians could not change it by anything they said. He went on to say that his men came from a seaport town and were Social Democrats—many had been Communists—"but I could not ask for better men," he said.

And now for those men who are not free, who are not allowed to read or listen to foreign radios, and who do not know why they fight. I remember in particular a little Russian prisoner, standing stiffly at attention in the dim light of the stone corridor, just outside the door of his cell. There was an iron cot, a mattress, a blanket, a chair. It was warm and he was comfortable enough. When we gave him a cigaret, he was still scared, and after he lit it, he would hold it stiffly down at his side as he stood at attention, and would raise his hand almost furtively to take quick, deep drags. He smoked it down until there was only a wisp of paper and a few shreds of tobacco. These he was afraid to toss on the stone floor as we did, but looked around with the cigaret coal burning his fingers, and finally put it right up against the molding.

The major who questioned him stood straight and erect, as a free man should. Because he had been an officer in their army in the old days when Nicholas II was Grand Duke of Finland, he spoke Russian well. His voice was direct but not menacing, and yet the man answered in a frightened dog's whine, the voice of a people who have been bullied by Commissars or Romanoffs and have cringed for centuries. It was several minutes before we could get him loosened up enough to talk. Finally he said yes, he had been told that the Finns killed all prisoners, and we understood this before the interpreter began, because he made slashing gestures across his belly as with a knife, and then from ear to ear under his chin.

They explained to him that I was a radio reporter and, his face lighting up, he said eagerly that he, himself, had seen a radio, and that some day the collective farm to which he belonged hoped to buy a radio, so all of them could hear it. We asked him how large his collective farm was, and he said it was two hundred forty families, about a thousand people.

We asked him if he was allowed to have animals of his own. He said he had had some chickens and a pig, but that things had got so bad last year on the collective that he had had to sell or eat them all. So now he had only his share in the collective. But once, he said, he had had many more chickens, and six pigs, and a cow, all his own. But of course this was before the collective, when he also had his own land.

We asked him which way he liked it better. He grinned sadly, shook his head, and said mournfully that there could be no doubt about this, he liked it much better when he had his own land, and his own animals and could look after all of them for himself.

Then one of the Finnish officers whose brother had been recently killed on the Isthmus, and who did not like Russians at all, told the interpreter to tell the man about the big Finnish victory in the north. The little man looked embarrased, with his eyes on our faces and then down, as though he did not know what he should say. Finally he said well, this was all right with him.

This answer satisfied the officer who did not like Russians. Then we asked him if he liked the food as well as that which he got in the Red army. Here his face lit up and he said it was much better, it was very fine food, with meat and potatoes and even white bread and butter. It was even better than the food he got at home. This pleased the officer very much.

Then he thanked us for the cigaret, which he said was a very fine one, and the interpreter explained that it came from America. But this the little man did not understand. So the interpreter said it came from the United States, which was a country. The little prisoner said when he had been in school he had heard the names of many countries, but could not remember that anyone had ever said the name of this country.

The very handsome Finnish major turned to me:

"At least, Mr. White," he said, "he has heard of Finland. This should be a very proud moment for our little country."

6

I SPENT the better part of a year in war-time Europe to learn just one salient fact. This is that democracy is not a substitute for determination and brains.

When I came out of Germany and Scandinavia into England and France, I was profoundly disturbed by what I saw. Yet in many ways I liked it, because these people were free and tolerant and open-minded as we are. They were enjoying to the utmost the things for which they thought they were prepared to fight —only they were not prepared. The atmosphere, after living in Germany, was as exhilarating as a release from prison—and no one who has been neither in a prison nor in Germany can know that this is not a hackneyed phrase.

It was very pleasant to find people free to read and to believe the idiotic accounts of the Finnish war carried by the *Daily Worker,* and to listen to the young British intellectuals discuss the skillful propaganda of Lord Haw Haw, the German announcer for the English programs from Berlin. The English, at that time, were too civilized and sensible to hate. By contrast I was glad to escape the organized and sustained malignancy of Berlin. And yet, at the back of my mind was always the doubt as to whether this fine academic tolerance might not be dangerous. I kept trying to persuade myself that organized hatred was not a useful weapon in war time. So when I looked at the freedom of England, I would be frightened and reassured by turns; reassured because it was so pleasant to be again in a free country where people could talk with their heads up and say what they thought without hissing it out of one corner of their mouth after first glancing behind them; disturbed when I saw the Peace Pledge Union handing out literature to all the young men called up for the draft; alarmed because these well-meaning intellectual fuddy-duddies had no remote conception of what was in store, not only for their empire and their island, themselves and their wives, but for the principles embodied in the leaflets, if the Nazis took over the island, because mercy and tenderness and love of fellowmen, with which these fuddy-duddies were overflowing and in which they were being encouraged by the German broadcast in English from Berlin, are not in the Nazi make-up, the Nazis having quietly and methodically butchered their own pacifists.

Yet the war, as it was being conducted under Chamberlain, before the occupation of Norway and the drive on the Channel ports, was very pleasant in England. The better bars of London were a kind of sartorial Aurora Borealis, only I had just come from Helsinki where a genuine war was still in progress and where the sartorial end was sadly neglected. The Finnish army had stopped worrying about how beautiful it looked. The boys began with good, substantial equipment but the shine soon came off their trench coat buttons after they had been dived on a few times when Russian shells came screaming over. The store creases left their trousers after they had been slept in for a couple of weeks straight. By contrast, the British were a Hollywood director's idea of what a well-turned-out army should look like, resting an elbow on a bar. In contrast to the Finns, they were men in uniform but not soldiers. I knew, of course, that this was only a matter of time, that the British had fought well in the last war and that a few million rounds of reasonably well-aimed German ammunition would presently turn them into troops. But that process had not yet begun. And there they were in the Berkeley Buttery, squiring exquisitely uniformed women of the various war services, for whom the London beauty parlors were then advertising different kinds of hair-dos, a special one for each type of uniform hat or fatigue cap, guaranteed not to muss.

There was the little British pilot on the train—he couldn't have been over 22—and very beautiful and cute he looked in his blue flyer's uniform.

Ribbentrop and Sir Nevile Henderson had just had a verbal interchange, and the result was in that morning's paper. Henderson's reply was ponderous and majestic and reeked of the stately homes of England. The little pilot was very proud.

"That's the sort of thing that makes one know there can be no doubt about the outcome," he said. "That's the strength of England—that we aren't represented by cads and bounders or rotters like Ribbentrop. That we have men of family and tradition—families dating back for centuries, to lead us—who have the wisdom of experience and can speak for England with dignity. That's what England's got that they can never have."

So what could you say? And of course I didn't say anything. But pretty soon the topic turned to aircraft. He wanted to know if I thought the German aviation was any good. He understood that most Nazis were abnormal—even encouraged that sort of thing. He couldn't think chaps like that would be any good in the air.

I said, cautiously, that I didn't think this was true—certainly it wasn't encouraged—and that I thought they had a very good air force. That maybe the English underestimated the rate at which the Nazis were building new planes—in addition to the ones they already had.

But at this point the kid interrupted me, politely and smoothly but very firmly brushed me aside. If what I said about the Nazis' rate of building planes was true, he assured me, I need not concern myself. Because naturally the proper people in England knew even more about it. They would have taken the proper steps. I could be very certain of that. He picked up his newspaper and began reading it, by way of dismissing me.

Now it isn't fun to be right. I'm sorry that those proper people, with wisdom and experience dating from centuries of those stately English homes which he trusted so much, turned out to be exactly the butter-fingered dunderheads that I suspected. Because he may by now have been filled full of steel and knocked out of the sky over Dunkerque or Hamburg or Dover as a result of his simple trust in them.

Last winter there was a good deal of talk going around among the British about their dogged endurance and staying power, while the intellectuals were busy re-making the continent of Europe. They were very open-minded. The mistakes of Versailles were to be avoided. The new democratic Germany, which would emerge after the Hitler regime had collapsed of its own weight, was not to be penalized, and a parliamentary federation was to usher in the new dawn. Disarmament was to be not unilateral but universal, and return of Germany's pre-First World War colonies was something you could discuss and many of these tolerant Britons were in favor of it. It was all very pleasant and relaxing after the organized venom of Berlin—except that you always wondered.

In France there was a great deal of disunity, which wishful thinking led you to discount as the native French aptitude for grumbling. The French conservatives were snarling back at the Popular Front for having toyed with the Russian alliance and for not having prepared. The French Socialists were surly toward the conservatives for having let a Fascist government get established in Spain and for using the war as a pretext to lower the hours and wage scales of French labor. They complained that the conservatives had rounded up and hustled all the Communists into concentration camps, while the leaders of the old Croix de Feu were still occuping high places in the army and the government ministries. French labor leaders were fighting to retain the forty-hour week. In the last desperate weeks they were to be working eighty-four hours a week to catch up on airplane production. But this proved to be too little and too late.

It was all there and yet you did not want to see it. The cracks which were to split France open were already visible. Railway service in this peace-time France which was only technically at war, was less dependable than it had been in Finland where the trains were frequently stopped for an hour so that passengers could run to the woods in safety from bombing planes. There was terrific confusion in the ministry of information. My French is a little better than reasonably good and yet it took me two days to find the proper official who censored press dispatches sent by clipper to America. I was misdirected and redirected for weary hours.

The American newspapermen were gloomy and they said the same dry rot of inefficiency was to be found in every ministry and that the army, even to the top, was just as bad. Only I kept repeating to myself the old litany that the French were a race of grumblers and that they had the best general staff in Europe and the largest body of trained army reserves.

In the bar of the Grand Hotel in Copenhagen in January, an American newspaperman who had just left Berlin told me that the Germans were planning to open a drive in the spring and that it would come around one or the other end of the Maginot Line, probably through Holland. This I had already written. So I asked the American newspaper boys about the conditions of the recent extension of the Maginot Line from Alsace-Lorraine to the Channel.

"It's in pretty fair shape," they said. "The British have been up there all winter, digging and stringing wire. They must have something to show for it."

"Aren't there any soft spots?"

"Well, yes, there is one. Just where the new line joins the old one, just opposite Luxemburg, the fortifications are pretty sketchy. Our guess is that they will come through there if they come at all."

Later, of course, they did, but while I was in Paris the shops were full of gay scarves and accessories on which were printed war maps of the Maginot Line for patriotic French women. These maps included the heavy fortifications along the Rhine and maybe areas of territory beyond it, back in Germany. Never did I see one which included the Channel ports or that soft spot behind Sedan—and it is hard to believe that facts which were then known to the American press section in Paris should be overlooked by the French General Staff as they were by the French couturiers.

I had been in both Paris and London shortly after the Armistice of the First World War, and the cities were full of ghosts. The same sandbags were piled around the base of Notre Dame; the same air raid sirens silhouetted on the rooftops against the chimney pots. You could almost think the same girls were doing approximately the same amount of business on the sidewalks between the Opera and the Madeleine. The same poilus' faces, resigned and philosophic, looked out at you from the windows of the troop trains as they slid by. But it was a land of ghosts, for victory was dead although we did not want to see it yet.

7

But now I would like to explain to my little American friends just why I am glad to be back here.

A few months ago I walked down a gangplank in New York, laid out my canvas bag and my knapsack for the customs officials and was very glad I didn't get charged duty on a tin hat and a gas mask. Now, of course, this is a very nice country, after seven months in warring Europe, but I'm not talking about its celery or olives or orange juice or its thick rare sirloins, or the fact that there is plenty of leg room in our taxis.

This country is nice in ways you know nothing about, my little pals, because you are so used to them. Ask any diver who unscrews his helmet to suck in a chest full of free fresh air.

Ask any correspondent who has come from the countries where

they are afraid to laugh, who has lived with people from whom all hope is gone.

Over here they won't believe you. They say, "Aren't you glad to get back here safe from shot and shell?" And the honest answer, which you only give to your best friends who might understand, is "Not particularly." Because you go over there to find out that there are things so much worse than shot and shell (which in themselves aren't particularly bad if they don't hit you or some one you know, and lots of fun to talk about afterwards) that a belt full of whistling machine gun bullets and a couple of personnel bombs can sometimes come as a great relief.

In point of hard fact the best time I had in Europe was in Finland where the air contained enough flying steel to satisfy everybody, and yet the Finns could always laugh and talk freely as they went about their business of sweeping up broken glass and mending busted railway lines and stringing barbed wire and filling sacks with sand. This was because, instead of giving up hope, they had decided to fight. A great many of them didn't expect to win. But they all knew it was better to fight, and have it end that way, than to go limp with discouragement and plod hopelessly through decades of darkness and defeat and cowardice.

The most unpleasant time I had in Europe was in Germany. "Yes, yes," my friends hasten to say, "the food must have been terrible." Now it happens that it wasn't. Usually it was just bad, and an occasional meal was good. Always there was enough—just barely enough, never plenty.

But you could get along, and I did (losing only four pounds) so that wasn't the trouble. The really unpleasant thing about Germany was the organized self-pity you met on every hand, and its consequences, which have yet to run their course. Now the dangerous thing about self-pity is that, in order to feel really sorry for yourself, you must eventually hate someone else. So the German genius for bothering other people (which we now see at its flower of perfection in Europe) rose from their original talent for snivelling.

Living in Berlin today is like living in a well-organized madhouse, run by its most pathological inmates, and dominated always by the echo of Hitler's venomously self-pitying scream. The few sane people you meet must whisper their sanities furtively, always looking over their shoulders to make sure that they are not overheard by some glittering-eyed swastika-bedecked madman, who will drag them off to a concentration camp where there are facilities for driving them crazy so that, upon release, they will work harmoniously with the rest of the population.

After a few weeks of this, it isn't only the ice water that you are glad to see again when you get back to America. It's the very simple fact that our people don't feel sorry for themselves. That they can smile without vindictive venom. And that a snivel which turns into a snarl is regarded as a pathological symptom, instead of the highest manifestation of the Racial Soul.

Coming out of Germany into the democracies was very little better. For here were very nice people dream-walking in the face of terrible danger. Preserving all the decencies and democratic amenities of life, and warfare, and diplomacy, against an enemy for whom ruthlessness was as much of a tool as a tank division.

When I arrived in England the Finnish war was just dragging to a close.

"Of course," explained the bright young Oxonian in the Foreign Office, "it's clear now that the Swedes and the Norwegians won't let us send troops across their territory to help the Finns. But if we were to do it by force—occupy Norway and Sweden to send troops there—(it would give us valuable bombing bases against Northern Germany) what would the reaction of American opinion be to that?"

So I thought. And then I said, "If you ask me that, I've got to say that American opinion wouldn't like it very well. But most of all, American opinion wants you to win this war. And if you must go through Norway and Sweden to do it, don't let anything else I say about American opinion stand in your way."

"But American opinion is very important to us," said the young Oxonian. "And then there's our own public opinion. Here we are, fighting a war to protect the small nations of Europe. Well, we can hardly start it by occupying two of them, what? Of course there's been some talk of doing it, but I don't think we'll ever go that far."

So they didn't. So in about a month the Nazis grabbed Norway, leaving Mr. Chamberlain with a moral victory. So from Norway's Stavanger naval base—which was within an hour's bombing range of Berlin—Nazi planes are now zooming off to bomb Scotland.

So another nice thing about this country is not just its ripe cantaloupes and other fresh vegetables, but also the fact that it isn't dream-walking over any precipices as England was under Chamberlain last winter. You may think we're not sufficiently aware of the danger. But with Hitler still some 3,000 miles away, we are registering all men up to thirty-six for military service, and with a little encouragement might raise this limit to 45. While last spring in England, with the Nazis only a few hundred miles away, they were doing business as usual with several million unemployed, and the upper limit of the draft was 27 years.

So the fact that we won't be caught napping is nicer than all the pieces of green apple pie à la mode in the land, although they are very nice.

But sweeter even than a breakfast of broiled pork tenderloin, fried hominy and coffee, is the justice we have in this country. You may think it can be improved. Or may never have noticed that it is sweet; this is because you've never been without it.

And so I can say to youth that I am glad to get back to a country and an atmosphere so fat and placid that it can afford the luxury of a disdainful skepticism about such stories as they filter in from abroad. A land where the honking juke boxes, in the little neon-lit dance places with comfortable booths, drown out the noise of screaming bombs. A land where youth is free to shrug its shoulders and say, "All this is none of my making, so why is it a responsibility of mine?" The only disquieting thing is that I saw shoulders shrugged with just this gesture in all the placid little neutral countries which war has since swept bare, or left ragged and smoking.

But most of all I am glad to get back here to find that our youth as a whole believes in freedom and self-government as deeply, and whole-heartedly as the youth of the Third Reich believes in the opposite. We actually believe, sincerely and almost naïvely, in what we are supposed to believe. But in those parts of democratic Europe which have come crashing down, by and large they didn't really believe in anything. Not even in their own right to order their own destinies. Some countries, of course, were just too physically weak to put up an effective fight. But, in too many of the countries people were too sophisticated, too civilized, too flabby. "How could it be much worse?" they would ask, with the inevitable shrug, without troubling themselves to make it better.

Watching them I would sadly conclude, over and over, that only back in America did we believe in our creed firmly enough and naïvely enough to match the naïve belief of the Nazis in theirs.

In the fallen democracies, they had shrugged away their ability to believe in anything, except, perhaps, the futility of all effort.

I hope some day there will come to our spinning little world an order and concept of life higher than the simple law of the jungle which the totalitarian states would impose on it. But I now know that the old concept will perish and the jungle will creep in on us, unless there are men who will rise as men have risen before, who are proud to fight and willing to die for this concept of freedom, as men fought and died and saved it in this country in the sixties.

And so I am glad to come back and proud to find that we have such men.

V

WE MUST ARM

Garrett Underhill

V

WE MUST ARM

I

The other authors of this book have presented their beliefs and the reasons for them. I will make no attempt to enlarge upon what has already been said. My purpose here is to demonstrate the necessity for serious military preparation and to show that it is not enough to be willing to fight for what you believe; you must know how to fight and be equipped to fight.

I do not intend to present an argument or to make an emotional appeal because I shall be dealing with simple conclusions from facts. I shall present certain occurrences from the past and from the present and I think there is only one set of conclusions that can be deduced from them. The easiest way to begin is to tell briefly four events from American history.

In 1813 the United States was fighting England in the war known variously as the War of 1812 and the War of Sailors' Rights. On the first of June, H.M.S. *Shannon,* a 38-gun frigate commanded by Captain Broke, was lying outside Boston harbor. Broke had been captain of the *Shannon* for seven years; he knew his vessel and he had trained his crew.

The *Chesapeake* of the tiny American navy put out from Boston to engage the *Shannon;* she had 38 guns and was physically the equal of the *Shannon.* The *Chesapeake* was commanded by Captain James Lawrence, an able captain and an excellent sea fighter, as he had proven on the *Hornet*. But he was newly in command of the *Chesapeake* and his men were raw. Because of the rash of privateers sailing under letters of marque, trained navy seamen were impossible to get. The third and fourth lieutenants and the first officer had seen no more of the *Chesapeake* than Lawrence himself had. Lawrence's orders were to engage the *Shannon*.

Lawrence planned to come down on the *Shannon* from windward, exchange broadsides, grapple and rake her. He gave his orders. Then as he bore down upon the enemy he found that his crew was not able to do what he told it. The *Chesapeake* had too much way on and the helmsman steered so close to the *Shannon* that the two frigates were practically aboard each other. Lawrence was trapped to windward, his forestays shot away, and with no chance to clear his ship and rake the *Shannon*. Broke was the one who turned his muskets on the *Chesapeake*.

That was about all there was to it. Lawrence, mortally wounded, ordered the call to repel boarders, but the Negro bugler threw his bugle overboard instead. The men and the officers fought and fought hard in groups and sections and twos and threes, and they died that way—brave, broken and demoralized.

Before he died, Lawrence gave a last order, in a military sense nearly his most important order, but in the confusion of disaster no one had experience enough to obey it. Lawrence cried out the words he is now remembered for, "Don't give up the ship! Sink her! Blow her up!"

On the fifth of July, 1863, an officer in Union blue walked over the battlefield of Gettysburg. He stopped in the middle of a group of Union dead and looked around. Across a fence in front of him lay a few bodies in Confederate gray, but the proportion was wrong; there were too many Union bodies.

The officer stooped and picked up a musket from the ground. The man who had used it, a young Irishman from his looks, lay at the officer's feet. He had been one of the new recruits. The officer cocked the musket and saw there was no firing cap under the hammer. When he pushed the ramrod down the barrel it did not go completely home and he knew that the gun was loaded. With a corkscrew device on the end of the ramrod, he probed the barrel and pulled out a bullet. He shook out the powder and tried again with the ramrod. In all there were three complete charges of ball and powder, unfired because no cap had been put under the hammer.

The officer moved on to another young soldier whose face was gone and whose arm was in shreds. The splintered stock of a musket lay beside the body. This had been another recruit and he too had forgotten what he had never really learned in training: how to load a musket. He had done what his companion did, but before a Confederate bullet hit him he had remembered, perhaps on the third or the fourth or even the fifth loading, to put a firing cap under the hammer. The gun blew up in his face.

This was not a new story to the Union officer; he had seen it happen many times. When a battle began there were one or two crashing volleys on order from an officer. Then organized volleys broke down in the smoke, the noise and confusion, and the men fired at will; the veterans regularly, precisely. The recruits tried to fire faster than their hands would let them and the rhythm was broken. In the pressure of battle they were not thinking human beings and musket fire was so new to them that the mechanics of it had not become habit. They had to think to remember the sequence of movements: select the cartridge, bite off the bullet, pour powder in the bore, drop in the bullet, ram the bullet home, put on the cap, full cock the hammer, put butt to shoulder, aim, fire.

The officer knew that if the process was not completely reflex motion, it was natural, even inevitable, that the men forget. It was natural, but he knew too that those who forgot might as well have gone into the battle barehanded.

On the twenty-third of June in 1898 at Las Guásimas, Cuba, Major General Joseph Wheeler wanted to make contact with the enemy. The troops under his command advanced through thick jungle on two converging roads. Wheeler himself commanded units of the regular army, units that had spent the last twenty years at tiny political posts engaged mainly in mowing lawns, units that even now were not used to maneuvering in formations as large as a battalion. Colonel Roosevelt, an amateur officer, commanded the Rough Riders, amateur soldiers.

Wheeler advanced down the main road and Roosevelt along the adjoining path. There was no plan; nobody had made a battle reconnaissance; nobody had so much as scouted the enemy position. But both columns wanted the honor of being first in face of the enemy, so they raced each other through the jungle. Neither column knew where the other was because no liaison was maintained between them.

Fortunately the Spaniards did not attempt to deal with each column separately. They remained on the defensive and were quiet even when Wheeler's regulars came into the open and began to deploy. Then a trial shot made the Spaniards open fire.

Colonel Roosevelt and his column were taken by surprise. The Mauser rifles kept on firing and men were dropping. The Rough Riders did not even know how critical their situation was; without liaison, under heavy fire from an enemy whose position they did not know and whose strength they could not determine, anything might have happened.

The column continued to advance blindly and at last joined Wheeler's troops. Under the circumstances the thing to do was to call for reinforcements, but Wheeler thought the honor of the troops was involved and he continued to sit and wait. Meanwhile men were being hit. At last a tactful suggestion persuaded him and he sent for help.

When the aid arrived there came the final humiliation. At first sight of the supporting infantry, the Spaniards departed. They had played with Wheeler; their plan had been to withdraw before the Americans came into sight, but they took the chance to inflict a few easy casualties.

Wheeler's performance had no military bearing, except possibly a negative one, on the outcome of the campaign. The result was that he lost sixteen dead and fifty-two wounded in carrying out an action that could have been accomplished without a casualty.

On the sixth of June in 1918 the 2nd American division was in the line near Bouresches. It was there because Foch had appealed to Pershing for any aid he could give to stop the drive of the crack German divisions that had broken his lines and were bursting and flooding deeper into France. The exhausted French were about ready to throw in the sponge when the 2nd Division moved in. Division orders came through that the 23rd Infantry was to attack at five that afternoon.

Before the war, the 23rd had been a regular regiment and one of the best, but it had been split to form cadres for two other regiments and then its own battalions had been filled to war strength with volunteers.

Still considered one of our best regiments, the 23rd sailed for France in September of 1917, and two-thirds of it spent the winter getting needed training while the other third built depots for the Service of Supply in the South of France. Before Foch's frantic call for help, the regiment had been in the now quiet sector southeast of Verdun, a poor preparation for what was to come.

On the way up toward Chateau-Thierry and Bouresches the men were undisturbed by the remnants of French streaming back crying, "La guerre, c'est fini." But the divisional, regimental and brigade staff officers were not so sanguine because they knew what bad staff work could do to even the best fighting force and they were aware of their own shortcoming. As in '98, officers who had handled anything as large as a peacetime battalion were fortunate. They knew little or nothing about the actual co-ordination of infantry and artillery.

Orders were late in coming through, but fifty minutes after the time set, the 3rd battalion moved into the wheat field to attack southwest of Bouresches. The artillery preparation had been inadequate because of lack of guns. A few one-pounders and machine guns did their best to keep the Germans quiet.

And the Germans were quiet as "K" and "M" companies led the battalion through the wheat field and the Springfield rifles opened fire. The battalion did not use any complicated tactics, just a straight frontal attack; very costly, but the only thing it knew. Then the heavy maxims from the German positions began to search the wheat from the front and flanks. They were steady and regular and their fire was planned. The Americans were pinned to the ground; even lying still meant death in a few moments.

Men began to filter back. When the battalion reassembled on the jump-off place, one-third of its strength was missing—eight officers and one hundred and sixty-five men. "K" and "M" companies were wiped out. And the attack had not gained one inch of ground.

Twenty-five days later, with the artillery concentrating its fire on the German gun positions and knowing more about what it had to do, the 3rd battalion attacked again through the wheat field under a low covering fire from one-pounders and machine guns that kept German heads down. The two assault companies went through the German lines, took their objectives, stood up under a terrific artillery bombardment, and repulsed a powerful counterattack. All this cost the battalion considerably fewer casualties than the unsuccessful attack of June sixth.

These four incidents were told not because they are important in themselves, but because they are examples of what it has cost us to do things the emotional and the unskilled way. These are not the only disasters in our military history; they are not even the important ones. These four minor tragedies can be duplicated a hundred times over in the records of the wars we have fought. There have been major disasters, too many of them, and some of our proudest victories can be more aptly described as useless slaughter.

I have picked these four cases because they are small and can be discussed briefly and because the reasons for what happened are more readily apparent than the reasons that bring about a great catastrophe, a catastrophe that stuns the mind by its very magnitude. The instances cited from four wars have this fact in common: men were trying to do what they did not know how to do. As a nation we have prided ourselves on the efficiency and skill with which we accomplish anything we set our hands to, but we have repeatedly put in the field troops that knew nothing about the job they were expected to perform. We would not expect a clergyman to use machine tools, but we have expected the untrained to do our fighting. War has always demanded skill, and today it demands far more than ever.

This nation in the past has paid a price for its wars in human life and money out of all proportion to the military results. Most Americans do not know this because the school history books speak of glorious and smashing victories and of a few defeats stubbornly contested by small bodies of men against overwhelming odds. Custer's last stand, for instance, has become a legend of heroism and the fact that it is a blot on our military history is largely overlooked. The facts about our wars are in the records, however, for anyone who cares to look. The lesson they teach is not pleasant.

It is not the purpose of this article to urge us into war or to plead for peace and I have no intention of doing either. It is true, however, that we have fought wars in the past, wars that we did not expect to fight, and what has happened before can happen again. Today the world is certainly not a safe place for the weak.

Men study history in large measure to learn how to avoid repeating the errors of the past. In these first pages I have gone back into our own history to show how we have suffered time and again from the same mistake. If this war comes to us, that mistake, repeated once again, will cost us a price in life and material resources from which we may never recover. I hope we do not run the risk.

In this connection, there is one last episode to be recalled from history. During our Civil War Napoleon III installed Maximilian of the house of Hapsburg as Emperor of Mexico and he kept him there with French troops. In 1866 after the end of the Civil War, Washington notified Napoleon that the presence of French troops in Mexico was a violation of the Monroe Doctrine and he would please remove them, or else. The veteran armies of the Union were not disbanded. Napoleon called his troops home. I mention this to point out that the only war for which we were ever prepared was the one we did not have to fight.

2

In the past, it is true, the United States has won its wars, and that is one reason why we, as a people, have been willing to accept and discount the consequences of being unprepared. If that were the only reason our attitude would be exceedingly difficult to understand, because no nation can expect miracles indefinitely and certainly no nation can afford to count on them. There are other reasons, however, and they are the ones I want to talk about.

Throughout the entire nineteenth century the United States was expanding on the American continent and was so situated geographically that it was able to incorporate into its domestic body politic the territory covered by its expansion. This tended to keep our minds occupied with our own affairs and to strengthen the already existing feeling of separateness from the rest of the world.

During that period we were as safe from outside interference and aggression as any nation ever has been. We were not haunted by the necessity to defend vital lines of communication and supply as were England and France, the two great colonial empires; we were not hedged about by powerful and often hostile nations as was Germany; we were not cut off from seaports as was Russia.

We had only two immediate neighbors and, after 1815, one was continually friendly. The other gave us trouble off and on, but it was never, by any possible stretch of the imagination, strong enough to be a serious threat. Leaving England out of the discussion for the moment, the possibility of invasion from abroad during the nineteenth century was so remote as to be negligible. Distances were reckoned in terms of weeks and even months so that the warships and supply vessels required to support even a small invading army were beyond all calculation. During this whole period, England was the only nation Americans thought of as a likely invader. Germany was not interested in America or in colonies at that time, and after Trafalgar France did not figure as a sea power.

England, however, had the sea power, she had Canada as a base of supplies and she had invaded us. During the Revolution, Burgoyne led troops down from Canada via Lake Champlain and New York State and he was defeated by Benedict Arnold at Saratoga in the battle that probably did more than any other to win the Revolution for the colonies. In the War of 1812 another British force invaded the United States, this time directly from ships, and burned the new capital city of Washington.

We did not like the experience of being invaded and until our relations with England became settled and permanently friendly we were afraid of Canada and of the Champlain valley in particular as the one great threat to our pleasant security.

But we began to find that we could adjust our differences with England and Canada. The English finally evacuated their posts in American territory around the Great Lakes and we later beat England to the Mexican possession, California. The agitation over "Fifty-four Forty or fight" was settled and England paid the *Alabama* claims arising from our Civil War. After the Canadian border was demilitarized, and Canada became self-governing, the evidence of these events helped to make us feel that England was our friend and that we were safe. At the time we were correct; England was the only power that could have hurt us.

As this brief discussion will show it is not correct to say, as many people do, that England has always held the Atlantic for us with her fleet and that that is the reason why we have never thought it necessary to have a two-ocean navy. In the first place, until after 1848 and the acquisition of California we only had one coastline to defend, and in the second place, until after the Civil War we wanted to keep what fleet we had in the Atlantic because of possible trouble with England. When we settled our difficulties with England we still had no need of a large fleet in the Pacific because Japan at that time was not a naval power. Russia was not a problem in the Pacific because her harbors were ice-locked a large part of the year. The building of the Panama Canal and the occupation of the Philippine and Hawaiian Islands near the turn of the twentieth century accurately date the time when we had to become a naval power in the Pacific. The tacit system of Anglo-American naval cooperation is even more recent.

There are three important points to be made about the position of the United States before the World War of 1914. All through the nineteenth century, when we were on good terms with England, we felt that we were safe from invasion; and we were. From 1812 to 1917 about the only real trouble we got into we made for ourselves. The reason we were safe was that distances were great and ships were necessary for invasion. England was the only nation that could invade us and she did not. We were safe because England refrained from attacking us. The corollary to this is, that as long as England remains dominant in the Atlantic she will be the only power with the ability to harm us. So long as England possesses the power to harm us we are secure, because she will never use it.

This I believe is the correct way of saying that England protects us in the Atlantic. The statement is true historically, as the other is not, and it suggests more accurately and less emotionally the inevitable results of the removal of British power. Of course there are other factors involved and I will attempt to discuss them, but they all stem from the fact that we trust England not to use her power against us.

In 1900, then, we were safe and now it is claimed that we are in danger. Why? What has changed our position? The question is very difficult to answer, not because the answer is unavailable, but because most of us now alive have seen the answer taking shape. In spite of the incredibly rapid changes of the past forty years, and of the past twenty-five in particular, we have not seen that those changes could be a threat to us in a military sense. We have been so close to change from day to day that it has not seemed like change to us; we have become so familiar with it that it has lost its meaning. It is only for the convenience of the historian that change takes effect at a given moment in time; the only way we can understand the importance of what has happened is to make a mental picture of what life was like for our parents and then compare it with a picture of our life today. To mention merely a few of the items that are always cited, the airplane, the automobile, the radio, movies, television and newspapers have brought about a revolution during the past forty years in the life of the individual and of society that is unequalled in history. It is necessary to realize the cumulative effect of the change that has taken place.

In 1900 if you set out for the Pacific coast from New York there was only one feasible way to get there, by train. It would take you upwards of a week. If you made the journey by any personal means of conveyance, you would be on the road somewhere in the neighborhood of two to three months. Those were the only methods of land travel there were. No motor roads existed as we know them now. Today that trip takes about twelve hours by commercial plane, twelve to thirty-six hours by private plane, between three and four days by train, and under a week by private automobile depending on how long and how hard the driver cares to drive. There are also busses that take only slightly longer.

In 1900 the average time for a trans-Atlantic crossing on one of the good passenger liners was in the neighborhood of ten days. Today the Clippers make it by air in about thirty-six hours and the service is so regular it is already a commonplace. The inauguration of air service to Europe has caused less stir than the record-breaking runs of the *Mauretania* more than twenty years ago. Think of this for a moment; it symbolizes the whole answer. And the difference in time is just forty years.

Translate this change in the peacetime life of society into terms of an equal change in military and naval science and you can readily understand why our geographical position no longer gives us safety.

Our security today depends upon the strength of England just as it did in 1900, but it depends upon that strength in a much more immediate and less reassuring fashion. At the end of the first World War Japan was just emerging as a strong military and naval power; today there are few nations so strong as she on land, on the sea, or in the air. In 1917 Japan was allied with England and co-operated with us; today she is more hostile than friendly to both England and the United States. In 1917, apart from having launched her twenty-one demands against China, Japan was still linked with the white nations in supporting the open door; today she claims to own China and the tenure of the Occidentals on the continent of Asia continues on suffrance by the Japanese. In 1917 there was no threat from Japan, but today the Philippines depend for whatever safety they have on the presence of the American navy in the Pacific.

In 1900 we depended on Britain in the sense that we trusted her not to do us damage. If by some peculiar alchemy England had been removed from the world, there was no other nation with the power and opportunity to injure us. But if Britain should fall tomorrow, even if her seapower should not go to Germany and we cannot safely assume that it would not, Germany would have the means to hem us in from the south and very possibly from the north. If we transferred our fleet to the Atlantic to meet the immediate threat, our possessions in the Pacific would be at the mercy of Japan or Russia. If England had fallen in 1900 we would have had ample time to prepare for any emergency, but if England fell tomorrow it would be a close squeeze.

It is not my place to answer the question, "Why would Germany want to invade the Americas?", nor is it my place to discuss the implications of the Monroe Doctrine. But I assure you that I am not summoning up bogeys when I say that unless we prepare thoroughly, with men and matériel, we will be up against it if England falls. So long as England keeps on fighting there is little that Germany can do about taking over South America or parts of it, but the groundwork is laid. Unless we were strong enough to do more than protest in words, Germany could take and maintain footholds in South America once England was out of the way.

I do not know that Germany would want to go into South America, but, victorious over England, she could if she wanted to. I emphasize this point because it is a popular belief, among other things, that bombers and transports cannot operate with full loads over a distance greater than a thousand miles and return. Nothing could be less true. The United States army flew loaded bombers a considerably greater distance in the remote past of 1937. Now nearing completion for the United States army is a bomber whose flight range is given as New York to Moscow and return to Los Angeles non-stop, with a load of bombs.

If England falls Canada will still be at war with Germany in her own right. This introduces another element of insecurity and hazard into the situation for the United States. In that case Canada will have the choice of continuing the war or of making peace on whatever terms she can get. If she elects to keep on fighting, the territorial waters of North America, the islands off the coast and Canada herself will become an active war zone. South America will have neither the means nor the inclination to prevent Germany from establishing military, naval and air bases, nor is there any reason to believe South America would not enter into economic and political association with Germany. Unaided, Canada's position will be so nearly hopeless as to make no difference, particularly if the British fleet is either lost to Germany or scuttled, and the United States will be more truly encircled than Germany ever was. If England falls and Canada makes peace, the only difference will be that the same result will be accomplished sooner.

People say in answer to this that the United States would never allow Canada to be defeated and that the Monroe Doctrine protects South America. The truth is that without complete and thorough preparation we would not be able to do a thing for Canada and the Monroe Doctrine would be interesting only as an historical document. With the best will in the world you cannot put untrained men with rifles and Teddy Roosevelt hats up against airplanes, tanks, machine guns and trained troops. Unprepared, the United States would not only be unable to help its neighbors, it would be desperately put to it to take care of itself.

People then say that the situation is not as bad as all this, that all that has been advanced here is assumption based on the remote contingency that England will fall. If you think the assumptions do not follow from the fall of England, I hope you will read Miss Mann's piece over again. In terms of military possibility the assumptions are very far from fantastic. If you think the fall of England unlikely, I ask you to think back over the list of nations that were considered unlikely to fall.

I agree that the situation is not as bad as this yet; this article is being written in the hope that it may never become that bad. Whether it does or not is largely up to us. There is little enough, in terms of large-scale aid, that we can do at the moment to help England, even if we want to; if we are interested in our own security, we must think of the possibility of a world without the British Empire.

It is difficult to picture such a world, but empires are not immortal. To the man of Cæsar's day the Roman Empire appeared as indestructible and as much a basic part of the world as the British Empire has seemed to us. But Rome fell.

We have been safe in the past and are safe now because England has been the only power able to do us harm. England invaded us from Canada once and a second time from the sea. If England falls, the power to do us harm will pass from England to Germany; Germany will assume the position in the Atlantic that England held for so long and she will have bases for possible attack on us certainly in the south and very probably in Canada. For the past hundred years we have trusted England not to use her power against us. To state it in the plainest, most realistic way, we could not trust Germany to take over England's position of power in the Atlantic and not use that power against us.

3

In this section I want to take up briefly the German military accomplishments and some of the reasons for them. The list of countries Germany has overcome is by now only too familiar: Austria, Czechoslovakia, Poland, Denmark, Norway, Holland, Belgium and France. These countries fell from the combined pressure of two different sets of causes; the things Germany did and the things they themselves did not do.

There is a myth growing currently to the effect that the Germans are invincible and it is just as untrue as the myth that flourished until the spring of 1940 that the Germans were overrated and could not stand up against the French army. The Germans have worked no miracles and they are not supermen and there is no mystery about what they have achieved. Raeder's navy, Goering's air force, and Keitel's army are the products first of fourteen years of planning and preparation and then of seven more years of hard work.

From the time of Frederick the Great, through Bismarck, and the first World War to Hitler, the Prussian military tradition has grown in Germany. After the defeat by the Allies in 1918, the German General Staff started a systematic study of every phase of the war to determine the reasons for Germany's defeat. The one great general lesson drawn from the study was that Germany lost when she failed to impose her method of fighting upon the enemy, in other words when she allowed the war to become stationary.

The research staff found among other things that the Allies credited their victory in large part to the individual initiative of their troops as opposed to the unquestioning obedience and lack of initiative of the Germans. If you recall, this was still supposed to be one of the great advantages of the Allies in 1939. But in the Field Service Regulations for the New German Army there is this passage: "War is the severest test of spiritual and bodily strength. In war, character always outweighs intellect. Many stand forth on the field of battle who in peace would remain unnoticed. In spite of technique, the worth of the man is the deciding factor . . . The emptiness of the battlefield demands independently thinking and acting fighters, who, considering each situation, are compelled to act boldly and decisively —determined to succeed."

Be it said the Germans did not slight the technique, but in view of this quotation the spectacular success of the German combat teams in Poland, Norway, Flanders and France is not surprising.

In Germany as soon after the last war as 1919, Prince Hubertus Loewenstein, a peace advocate, reported seeing boys armed with staves maneuvering across fields and woods, practicing infiltration tactics and short rushes. Multitudes of bronzed German youths began to swing along the country roads and upland pastures in full pack and the government helped set up Youth Hostels so that boys engaged in the "defense sport" of group hikes could get accommodations for the night.

Treaty stipulations limited the German army to 100,000 men, but General Hans von Seeckt made of the crack Reichswehr a kernel from which a large army could grow. Junior officers and non-commissioned officers were to come from it. In Germany there was no opportunity for senior officers to handle large bodies of troops so many of them went on loan to Russia and China to get the practice they needed. At home the police force was militarized, there were private and political armies, and organizations of technical war specialists concealed under odd names.

Although Germany was not allowed to make arms for herself, she exported them and kept her factories in production. The Republican government set up a special department of aeronautics and aerial transport that superintended all air activities. The *Deutscher Luftsport-Verband* watched over the innumerable air clubs all over Germany. Air transport was heavily subsidized and in 1925 it was unified into one line, the Deutsche Luft Hansa. By 1930 the DLH was operating ninety different runs with a total of 90,000 kilometers daily flying. Inside Germany its runs were short and numerous; abroad it flew planes to London, Stockholm, Oslo, Paris, Budapest, Barcelona, Belgrade and Constantinople. Its reconnaissance flights reached the Far East. Each year the DLH took a large share of the

50,000,000 marks that was the average yearly aviation subsidy of the Republic.

Germany was not allowed to build military planes, but outside the Reich German factories regularly built and tested them. The Stuka of today—Junkers Ju87—was designed and flown in 1930 as plane K-47 from Professor Junkers' plant in Malmo, Sweden. On Lake Constance in Switzerland Dr. Dornier experimented with bombers and fighters.

Beginning in 1925 commercial pilots' licenses could be obtained only at the Reich's flying school. It took four school years to get a pilot's certificate and two or three years to become a lower-rating combination pilot and mechanic.

Hitler did not start entirely from scratch. He had the skeleton parts of his organization to hand, ready to be put together. As soon as Goering took over as air minister under Hitler, he began the job of channeling the previous efforts. Nothing was too good for the air force. New factories were begun in safe locations, they were well tooled and were equipped with underground duplications of the entire surface setup. Great districts in Western Germany were declared verboten; hillsides were sheered away, hangars put in and the landscape restored so that not even before-and-after photographs would reveal the change.

By 1935 the air force could not be concealed any longer so the German "sports enthusiasts" climbed into Heinkels and Arados and became the Richthofen and Horst Wessel pursuit squadrons. The 1930 tri-motored Junkers transports of the Luft Hansa were used by the bomber groups. The Dornier pre-Hitler DO-23 "freight carriers" turned out to carry bombs as well. But Goering was still the funny man of Europe and no one took his air force seriously. It was not until 1937 at the Zurich air meet that Goering showed anything of what he had in hiding. There the DO-17, the "flying pencil," took the bomber prizes for load, speed, and range; the earlier versions of the Messerschmitts took prizes in the fighter classes.

Meanwhile the compulsory labor classes begun in 1933 were turning out hard, fit men. In 1935 Hitler incorporated 300,000 men from the year's labor class into the regular army. The skeleton frame of the Reichswehr was beginning to take on flesh. Foreigners did not believe Germany could build an army short of a decade or so, but determination, slashing of red tape and the dodges practiced before 1935 helped get the job done.

By 1936 Germany was ready for a dress rehearsal. Junkers air transports that later flew troops to Vienna ferried General Franco and his Moors across the Strait of Gibraltar. Test squadrons of Heinkels, Messerschmitts, Dorniers and dive bombers tried out all their tricks in Spain and then photographed the results so that corrections could be made. Light tanks turned out to be vulnerable, to throw their tracks and to be ill-armed. In Germany alterations were instantly made at the assembly lines and heavier, better armed tanks were the result.

Things were not rushed. The Spanish war was prolonged so that more German troops could find out what war was like. U-Boat Commander Prien learned at the expense of Loyalist merchantmen the skill he later used to sink the *Royal Oak*. Speed boats that were to raid the English Channel patrolled the Spanish coast; German naval officers served on Nationalist cruisers and destroyers. Then when the time was come the Italians and the Germans smashed the Loyalists in a series of envelopments that were blueprints for the campaigns in Poland and Flanders.

By 1938 the number of anti-tank guns included in a German division was seventy-two. The French had less than fifty-four. Germany had been successful in Spain with 37 mm. anti-tank guns, but because of the extra power it was decided to use 47 mm. guns. France had a gun that encounters in Spain had proved useless, but she faced the Nazi tanks in the spring of 1940 with the same impotent Hotchkiss.

After the Spanish war, Germany was ready. Errors and defects revealed in Spain and in maneuvers were ironed out. By July of 1939 the German army had one hundred and twenty-four divisions against eighty-three for France and England. Italy had an additional sixty-three divisions.

In short Germany has drilled and planned and arranged her forces for the way they were to strike. Her men have been trained for their job and have had accurate maps of the areas they were to fight in. They practiced crucial operations at home on dummy battlefields and beaches. They have been able to dictate the conditions under which the fighting has taken place. They have exploited to the fullest the principles of economy of force and concentration. They have obtained the most out of the least by knowing what they were going to do.

That is a résumé of what Germany has done. The story of what the Allies have not done is the other side of the picture. The great weakness of the Allies, and of the United States, was that they were not willing to look an unpleasant situation in the face.

After the last war, the British military scholar Liddell Hart wrote two books, *Europe in Arms* and *Defense of Britain,* in which he set forth the military theory that England and France have operated on ever since. He maintained that the power of arms had come to a point where a strong offense would fail if thrown against fortifications supplemented by small and efficient defense forces. France built the Maginot Line and England decided that it would be unnecessary again to send a large expeditionary force to France. It was thought that any war would be won by attrition through superior economic resources.

The doctrines of Liddell Hart have turned out to be false as practiced, but his doctrines themselves may still be sound enough. He was careful to specify that defense must be efficient and that then it can overcome odds in numbers of three to one. That is the joker. England and France saw that offense in the terms of 1914–18 was doomed to failure and neglected to observe the necessary condition. They did nothing to make their defense efficient and they did nothing to prepare a defense for the kind of fighting they might have to meet. What was going on in Germany was obvious, but neither England nor France saw it because neither of them wanted to. They refused to believe that if you are preparing defenses, you must be ready to meet the actual power your possible enemy has and not the power you hope he has or that you think he ought to have.

The popular attitude in France and England and the United States was one of complete self-delusion. It is evidenced by the reports that supposedly competent and well-informed observers sent back to this country. The reports were read joyously and with faith. Informed comment in this country was just as misleading.

In one case it is amazing to see that one writer had hold of the truth and turned it around into falsehood. In December, 1938, the Report of the Foreign Policy Association said, "It is difficult to believe that Germany has created a first-line air force of 10,000 planes, all organized and ready to take off. . . . Moreover, unless a nation is deliberately building against a prearranged date at which it intends to begin a war, it is unwise to assemble any great number of planes in the present state of aeronautical science; for planes are being improved so rapidly that today's miracle is obsolete tomorrow."

There were men who knew and who reported the facts, aircraft engineers from this country like Bell, Kindleberger, S. Paul Johnson and T. P. Wright who had been to Germany, Italy, England and France. But nobody listened to them.

Just before Germany went into Poland people here and in Europe were reading and believing things like the following quotation from an article entitled "Germany Can't Win" in the June, 1939, issue of the *American Mercury.* "Today one may confidently state that the German army could not fight the French single-handed, with any genuine hope of success. . . . Sum it all up and it comes to this: *Germany cannot win a war of one begins today, tomorrow, this year.*"

On the 15th of the preceding December in a *Foreign Policy Report* the same author wrote, "All this marks the passing of the old Blitzkrieg idea in which a lightning attack was to burst through the French defense lines and to overwhelm the *troupes de couverture,* accompanied by a mass air attack on Paris. Germany now plans to remain on the defensive in the West, and proceed with its eastward expansion, facilitated by the bloodless defeat of Czechoslovakia."

In the *New Republic* of May 24, 1939, he said, "While striving in the East to overwhelm Poland, the Germans might assume the defensive as to France. . . . Against the full weight of the French army they might hope to hold for some weeks; but not by any means indefinitely . . . Poland could fight a long, delaying war . . ."

It wasn't very long ago. Does any of this sound familiar?

In the issue of June 12, 1939, one of our great weekly magazines said that although the situation was not the same as directly after Munich when "General Marie Gustave Gamelin, France's chief of staff, assured his government that he could roll his men through the unfinished German Siegfried (or Limes) Line like marmalade" in any event "the French army was still the strongest all-round fighting machine in Europe."

False information of this kind has continued to be believed ever since. When Germany went into Norway we agreed with Chamberlain that Hitler had overreached himself at last. Our press was telling the public on April 22, 1940, that while "the situation of the German forces in Norway is not desperate, the critical need is for immediate reinforcement." And on April 29, "The British navy, by use of submarines and mines, has made precarious German sea communications across the Skagerrak." Just before that on April 10, headlines in the New York *World-Telegram* announced that the "Second Battle of Jutland rages on sea and in the air." The New York *Journal and American* ran a drawing of a battle between British cruisers and German vessels of convoy showing destruction of the Germans. No such battle ever took place. In the end the German victory in Scandinavia came as a bitter surprise to the democracies who had spent the winter in sloth and chest-puffing.

It was not until after Chamberlain fell that England announced it was putting airplane production on a seven-day week with multiple shifts. France had never bothered to move her airfields, her vital war industries, or her supply stations into safe places away from the vulnerable Paris area. When the great air attack on Paris began, the press immediately claimed that the raid was a failure because civilian casualties were low. The fact was that France was already crippled; the German bombardiers were systematically wrecking the airfields, the great airplane factories on which France depended for virtually all her planes, and the armament plants.

In the early thirties France was the strongest military power in the world. The German military machine was as yet no match for the French, but even then France's equipment was old. Her artillery was largely held over from the last war. She did not want to change her equipment because she felt that in a few years the replacements would in turn need replacing. She would not listen to her young officers who urged new methods and new kinds of weapons. When the pinch came she had nothing she could use; just a few scattered pieces of new material. There was no steady supply coming in. She had thousands of old planes that were as out of date as a model-T Ford and she had to start from the beginning on her air force. England had nothing except her navy and some twenty divisions neither fully trained nor equipped.

That in outline is the story of why Germany has had her way in Europe. With German determination and work on one side and Anglo-French unwillingness to see danger and do what was needed to meet it on the other side, the result is not surprising. I repeat there is no mystery or secret about the German success and the Allied defeat. If we had not hidden our heads in the sand, we would have foreseen it. In war as in politics, or anything else, you can't beat something with nothing.

4

In the United States there has always been a large body of belief firmly opposed to the creation of an adequate military establishment during time of peace. It is held that an army in peace time is unnecessary, that it is contrary to the democratic ideal and that it is a danger to the democratic state.

This belief cannot be brushed aside or ridden over rough-shod, because it is an honest belief and to do anything of the kind would be to inflict a serious injury on democracy. It must be explained and shown false.

The belief was first given general expression in the debates and controversy that preceded the adoption of the Federal Constitution in 1789. Here in passing it should be pointed out that the military needs of a nation of 130,000,000 persons, occupying a continental area roughly 3,000 miles by 2,000 and possessing outlying territories almost as extensive again, cannot be defined in the same terms as those of a nation of less than 10,000,000 occupying only a narrow strip of seaboard.

The men who framed the Constitution and the Americans of the late eighteenth century were desperately afraid of what they called factions. Today we would call a faction a special interest group or a political pressure group. The Constitution was designed so that no one branch of the government could act over the veto of either of the other two branches. This was aimed to prevent any one man, or group of men, in the government or out, from running the nation for his, or their, own personal advantage.

At that time an army was regarded as a possible political force and so as a danger. It was thought that an army might by threat of force compel the government to do its will, that under an ambitious commander it might take over the government, or that it might be induced to do either one of those things by a powerful private clique. This fear was not unfounded as history and the present situation in Japan both demonstrate.

But the army they were talking about was a different animal from the one we want and need today. An army at that time was made up of men who enlisted for long periods of time and who became professional soldiers. It was a case of once a soldier, always a soldier. That system also led to the creation in many countries of an hereditary officer caste. A large standing army of that kind could acquire a consciousness of self as distinct from the national community, and it could develop continuing political and and social interests dangerous to a democratic state.

Now we have never had an officer caste and the method of selection for West Point and Annapolis ensures that we never will. We need a regular army as a nucleus, as we always have, but, we do not want a large, long-term enlistment, standing army.

The idea of the Nation in Arms or the Citizens' Army is democratic in origin; it began in France at the time of the French Revolution. Napoleon used the idea for his own ends; but at that time France preferred glory to democracy; she was in much the same physical, mental and spiritual condition as Germany in 1933. Napoleon's enemy Metternich, the great reactionary, autocratic chancellor of Austria, knew that Napoleon could be defeated only if he built Austria's armies on the principle of the Nation in Arms. He knew too that if he did, the absolute Austro-Hungarian monarchy could not survive. He built his armies on the new democratic idea, he helped defeat Napoleon, and he saw the upsurge of democratic feeling break him and his Continental System.

From 1871 through 1940 the Third Republic of France was a democracy and through that entire period it employed the idea of the Citizens' Army. It is not the fault of that system that France is no longer democratic. The history of Switzerland is identified with universal military service and there are no more democratic people than the Swiss.

In the United States we have at several times had large armies. We have had them after wars instead of before, but supposedly the danger of an army to a democracy is greater at such a time. We have had generals as Presidents, but the army has never voted such Presidents into office or forced them on the nation. We have had two great organizations of veterans, one after the Civil War and one after the World War. They have acted as groups on several occasions, but they have never put forward one of their own number as their own political candidate and they have never exercised any important political pressure by using their voting strength as a group. The one great example of pressure brought by a veterans' organization is the Bonus March and that was unofficial. It was also democratic in intention, if messy in performance.

The system by which a nation calls on its young men of a certain age each year for a limited period of time for military service and by which in time of crisis it calls on all its trained manpower is completely and essentially democratic. We could not embark on such a program now if we wanted to because time is too short. We need more men quickly than such a plan would give us. But in time of peace, in time of crisis, or in time of war either universal military service or the selective draft is democratic. From the point of view of the military services or from the point of view of the civilian there should be no words bad enough to describe volunteering.

The American army or navy officer is not a militarist; he does not want war nor does he want to organize the country on military lines. He is trained and paid out of the taxpayers' money to be a public servant. He is not a loafer; he has a job to do. If he wants to remain in the army or the navy, he has to work. He is trained and competent, but he cannot perform miracles. In other words he is a human being.

It is the job of the officer to know his business, to know and understand the military risks that face the country and to make it his responsibility that there are methods ready to meet any military possibility. We train him and pay him to do that job and then when we need his advice we don't listen to him. We have always preferred, and we seem still to prefer, amateur opinion. If you have a toothache you see a dentist; if you want a picture painted you see an artist; if you want a plan for a building you see an architect. We want a plan for defense; we should see the army and navy before we buy anybody's patent panacea.

But the services cannot give a plan of defense unless they know what is to be defended. It is not the function of the armed services to formulate national policy and neither the army nor the navy has ever attempted to do it. But unless there is a national policy, there can be no efficient defense. Today no one knows what the nation is committed to. There is wild talk of every description and phrases like "national defense," "continental defense" and "hemisphere defense" are thrown around indiscriminately. Each of those phrases sets up a completely different military problem.

Over the past year as the crisis in the world has grown more desperate and the United States has veered from one line of action toward another, the staffs of the army and navy have worked night and day preparing detailed defense plans suitable to each shift. Such a plan, to be any good, takes months and, in quiet times, often years of intense labor and it must be scrapped with any change of national policy.

We are now engaged on a vast program of rearmament. Because we are doing it all at once it will cost us many times what it would have cost us if we had done it over the past twenty years. That, however, is water over the dam. In spite of the current feeling that you can produce planes, tanks, guns and ships merely by appropriating money, it will be 1944 or later before we receive all the equipment we now have on order. In turn that equipment will be of no use to us when we get it unless we have trained men to use it. You can't get trained men just by saying, "Train some men"; it takes time and planning and effort. But assuming that we get both equipment and trained men, in case of war the whole colossal effort can go for nothing unless we know exactly what we are going to defend.

In war the defender has a certain advantage. Provided that his fortifications are strong and his troops efficient, he can defeat a considerably stronger attacking force. But there his advantage ends and his disadvantages obtain equally in the air, on the sea and on land. He must spread his forces and be ready to meet an attack at any point. The attacker can devote all his training to making his troops ready for an assault on certain terrain, he can concentrate his available forces for an attack on one point of his own choosing, and, most important, he can pick the time and place most favorable to him and most unfavorable to the defender.

Defense is quite possible, but it is not easy. If there is any doubt about what is to be defended, if the plan of defense is too hastily made, if there is any improvisation of facilities at key points, if there is any lack of equipment or trained men, if there is any confusion about what is to be done or what has to be met, then the error is likely to be disastrous.

It is true, of course, that any plan of defense is contingent not only on what we want to defend but also on what we have time to prepare for. We must build and we must train and we must make up our minds about what we want our national policy to be. Let us make up our minds what we would like eventually to be able to defend from attack and then let us take the problem to the men we have trained to deal with it. It will be their job then to tell us how much we can defend at any given point in our preparation program, against any given attack. Knowing the direction of our policy and its ultimate scope, they can prepare plans that will be workable in terms of the state of our preparation at any moment along the way and that will also tell us how much we must do to defend ultimately everything we wish to defend.

All this sounds like a large job. It is a large job; it is also long and exacting. It will take work and devotion and determination, but it is not impossible. We know that we can build the equipment if we have time because we know how to do it. We can find out what we have to do to defend ourselves by making up our minds about what we have to defend.

The thing we know least about is training men. The American knows a good deal about the results of war and he has a hatred of the terror, the destruction, the horror and the deliberate brutality of war, but he knows very little about what goes into the making of a soldier when that becomes necessary. In that connection, the most informative thing to say is that the German units are not called *combat teams* by accident. The German army is organized on the basis of small units, each acting independently as a co-ordinated part of the whole. The members of the units are trained together and they practice together as a team. Each man in the unit plays his own position; he knows the other members and he knows in what characteristic manner each one will carry out his own assignment.

In this country every year we turn out thousands of highly skilled, magnificently trained combat teams, both professional and amateur. They happen to be football teams, hockey teams, baseball teams, or basketball teams, but the principle is the same.

Americans have no continuous military tradition, but they have a strong athletic tradition. We have physical and mental aptitude in high degree for bodily and team contests. We also have mechanical skill in equally high degree. Understand me; I am not saying that because a man can drive a car he can operate a tank, nor am I saying that the battle of Waterloo was won on the playing fields of Eton. Nothing could be farther from the truth. In fact, in many cases, it is easier to teach a man who has never driven a car how to operate a tank than one who has driven cars all his life. The reason is that the first man has nothing to unlearn. I am not advocating drafting athletes, but I want to point out that if we applied to training our army the skill, the effort and the discipline that every year goes into making athletic teams, we would go a long way toward a trained and skillful fighting force. People that as a nation can learn the fine points of team play can learn to be efficient soldiers if they wish to. The skills are not the same by a great deal, but they are similar, and they can be taught by similar methods.

The success of a team depends on the quality of its human

material, the excellence of its coaching, and the intelligence with which it is directed. The success of a fighting force depends on exactly those factors and one more—equipment. We have the human material for our fighting forces, as good as there is anywhere, and we can get the coaching, the intelligent direction and the equipment if we will keep our heads and plan and work.

That is the size of it and we must do it now. I have not talked in this article about the immediate practical difficulties of the army and the navy. There are many of them and they should be known and understood by the public. They can be dealt with and solved, however, if the nation is of a single mind about what must be done.

In the past we have not been prepared for any of the wars we have fought and we have paid a terrible price because of it. The only war for which we were prepared we did not have to fight. Today we can no longer depend on our geographical situation and on the distribution of power in the world to give us safety. Germany has succeeded so far because she was strong and determined and because the Allies were undecided, blind and weak. If I have been able to demonstrate those points then the conclusion follows that if we do not want to run the military risk of going the way France went, we can afford to be neither undecided, blind nor weak.

In conclusion I'm going to say something that is outside the scope of this article, but which, as the author, I would like to say. The German state of today is organized on the belief that war is not only one of the legitimate activities of the state, but that it is one of the ends for which the state exists. The function of the human being is to serve the state and he is trained to believe that war is the highest form of activity. The sum of the human beings in Germany does not equal the state; the state is greater than all the people that make it up; it has an existence of its own and its purpose is to aggrandize itself, not to benefit its citizens.

The theory of this democracy is that the state exists for the benefit of the people who make it up; that war is shameful, criminal and degrading; that the human being has rights of which no one can deprive him. If we build an army, an air force and a navy, we must do it on the conviction that democracy and freedom as we have known them and as we hope to improve them in the future are worth anything we have to go through to keep them, including war if that is necessary. We must not imitate the German system to meet the threat. If we compromise with our idea of what the United States should be, then an army cannot help us.

VI

THE FAITH OF AN AMERICAN

WALTER MILLIS

VI

THE FAITH OF AN AMERICAN

What follows is an essay in autobiography. While a generation of young Europeans was growing up amid the catastrophes which Erika Mann describes, a generation of young Americans was finding itself more distantly involved in the same historic processes. We looked on, more or less consciously, at the European revolution; more or less consciously we saw our own notions of society and our convictions about our world shaped or modified by its dimly apprehended lessons. We, also, made our mistakes; though so far they have exacted less ferocious penalties. We, also, learned something perhaps by experience, and though it is true that one's own experience will never teach another, an account of how many of us thought and felt under the impact of the great changes of the past quarter of a century may be not without its interest for those younger men and women who have so often cited us as supporting witnesses—or as horrible examples.

How far I may be typical of what came to be called the "Lost Generation" I do not know. Precisely because I bear so few of the conventional stigmata, I may actually be more typical than one would suspect. So far as I know, I was never "lost"; but then, very few of my contemporaries seem to have been either. Though I was in uniform during the World War, I never saw a battle; and though I was in Paris from time to time after it, I never sat at length with Hemingway expatriates on the terrace of the Dome or the Select, engaging in endless, monosyllabic dialogues in disillusion. But in these things I suspect that I am by no means unique. I have had much less direct experience of war than many of my age; to some extent, however, this is counterbalanced by the fact that my professional interests have required me to read and think about it rather more, probably, than most. War, at all events, has formed the ultimate background of my entire active life. Either in its prosecution or its preparation, in its physical horrors or its broader social implications, it has constituted a framework dimly surrounding all other activities, affecting every idea of the purposes of our society, limiting in one way or another every vista of the international or domestic scene. And in this I am not different from any other American in his or her early forties.

The first impact of war on my own consciousness was the romantic one. I was fifteen when the Great War broke over Europe; and it broke with a glamor which the present struggle can scarcely exercise, I imagine, over any fifteen-year-old of today. The vast present literature of mud-and-blood did not then exist. I had seen pictures of contorted corpses in *The Photographic History of the Civil War*; but that work, vivid as it was, conveyed nothing like the pain and futility which darken every page of Stallings' *First World War*. The soldier of my imagination was still a Kipling or a Richard Harding Davis character; and though something of the horrors might look out occasionally through what I had read about the Napoleonic, the Civil or the Spanish-American conflicts, they had been long dimmed by time.

Boys of the same age today have had, I suppose, a much sounder education in the grim subject. I got mine slowly, and with what now seems to me an almost incredible naïveté—until I realize that this very naivete, which was a product of the censorships and which was shared by grown men and women as well as by children, was one of the significant differences between those times and these. Up until the very end, when the Armistice found me just finishing my preliminary training and with a very raw second lieutenant's commission in my locker trunk, I had never, in all my imaginings as to what "it" would really be like, achieved any picture remotely approaching the reality. Something of the glamor of militarism persisted; and I remember my own shock when, proudly presenting myself to my mother, as a "surprise," in my new officer's uniform, I suddenly saw by her face that to her it was like my death warrant. I had not thought of that side of the matter. I was still picturing myself as a story-book soldier. I was still imagining myself swinging a field battery into action with all the dash and drama of a parade-ground manoeuver. I was as raw as that.

But I was not carried away by what afterward came to be called "war hysteria." Perhaps some of my classmates were. A number dropped out early to join up for active service; one or two were killed, several others made war records of great distinction. I wondered a little at the time as to the exact motives by which they were impelled—and I still wonder occasionally. Partly, perhaps, they were swept away by the excitement and the propaganda. But others of us, even then, entertained our doubts; and they were no different from the doubts besetting younger people today. I was, of course, afraid; I may have had no conception of what the Great War was really like, but by 1917 hints were beginning to come through the censorships. If there was still a great deal of the Arthur Guy Empey kind of literature about, there was also Barbusse by that time and a terrible little book, *Men in War,* by the Hungarian, Latzko. I was afraid of being afraid. And I was skeptical. No one with the slightest bent toward an analytical attitude could fail to feel that the propagandas were overdone, the causes of the war obscure, its promised gains uncertain. We were all "liberals" in those days, and believers in the rational life. I remember my inner conviction—running like a thread under the "Squads right!" and the nomenclature of the three-inch field gun—that no people could possibly be so wholly given to rapine and slaughter as the Germans were represented as being. The immediate cause of the American entry into the war—the submarine campaign, which had actually taken only a handful of American lives—seemed somehow inadequate; the menace of a German invasion of the United States, with which this cause was buttressed, seemed far-fetched and always rather unconvincing; the greater aims of winning a war to end war and of making the world safe for democracy were much more moving—but I remember that I doubted even then whether they would in fact be realized.

So far as I can recall, it was no sense of burning consecration, no fanatical devotion to a leader or a cause, which overbore these rational doubts and carried me down a path which, save for the ending of the war, would have dropped me unresisting into the agony of the Western Front. It was, rather, a matter of drifting with the tide. I was simply one of my kind, doing as they did, accepting the role for which the social framework of which I was a part had cast me. I did not offer myself heroically before I was called; I never, on the other hand, had any impulse toward the part of a conscientious objector. Possibly I was politically and socially more immature than the better-educated youths of today. Afterward, at any rate, it seemed to me that this was an irrational and unsatisfactory way in which to go down into the terrible vortex of modern war. To enlist for killing without a deep conviction—or without a signed, sealed and delivered contract to guarantee that the sacrifice would be worth while—seemed the height of foolishness; to offer up one's life to a cause simply for the reason, at bottom, that everyone else was doing it seemed a grotesquely childish proceeding. So it often appeared to me afterward. But today I am not so sure; and much of what follows is by way of explaining why I am not sure.

What kind of soldier I would have made, with this emotional equipment, I was never to learn. At the time I hoped that I would do my duty when the crises came; I still hope that I would have done it. I do not know. But in general (neglecting whatever personal reactions the stress of battle might have brought out in myself) it seems to me that this way of going to war is not a bad foundation for the soldierly virtues. I suspect that men who have enlisted because everyone else is doing it—because, in other words, there is a group job to be done and they are part of their group—are better equipped to stick it in the long run than men driven by such suicidal fanaticisms as the Nazis inculcate in their shock troops, or even than men impelled by great ideals which, in this imperfect world, are nearly always doomed to stultification. I suspect that the front-line soldier who fights because he is there, because his immediate comrades are fighting, because he cannot let down the squad on his left or right or abandon the infantry being covered by his tank guns, will fight better and longer than those guided by less simple, more lofty, more logical and therefore more vulnerable motives. This is, of course, no answer to the question of whether one should fight at all or not. But it contains, perhaps, a hint of the answer. And I found a similar hint in my own feelings as I looked back on it after the war was over. I never for a moment regretted the fact that chance had spared me the suffering and horrors of the battlefield; I was never bothered (even in the earlier post-war days, before we had all grown so cynical over the results) by the thought that I had struck no blows for the new world of peace and democracy. But what I did regret, even while I was glad that I had escaped, was that I had missed one of the great experiences of my generation. An immense and terrible task was performed by my contemporaries. I would have liked to have had a share in the doing of it, quite regardless of what was done. It was a part of the heritage of my age, of the society, the group, in which and by which I lived. I would not have done it for fun; but since, historically, it had to be done, I would have liked to have had a share in it. And therein there lies a real hint, I think, not only of the reason why men do fight but of the reason why, at times, they should.

But none of us was thinking about fighting again in those days. We had all suddenly been dumped out into the peace of 1919. The war to end war had been won at last—and for millions of men and women it really had been a war to end war, in spite of all the cheap sneers that have since been flung at that phrase—while few even of the most skeptical among us could have imagined that in fact they would ever live to see another like it. Some of us, as I have said, had found out in the hard way what modern war really is; the rest of us were soon to learn. I forget when Philip Gibbs's *Now It Can Be Told* first blossomed in the bookstores, but no one who had reached the age of literacy in the earlier nineteen-twenties is ever likely to forget the long and terrible procession of the war books which followed on its heels. Perhaps they made a deeper impression upon those who had not been there than upon those who had. I am rather struck by the fact that among men of my acquaintance it is those who saw active service in the last war who are, as a rule, the strongest supporters of a bold foreign policy today and the most ready to risk their lives again if such a policy should fail to avert a conflict; while the man who has made himself the chief national spokesman of the policy of appeasement, safety and scuttle is Colonel Lindbergh, who was too young to take part in the last struggle. But the World War, as experienced either directly or in the vast testimonial of pain and courage, horror, suffering, fortitude, weariness and disillusion which it produced, has left on all men and women of my age an impression which is ineradicable.

It is not surprising that for so many of us the strongest impulse that we brought to the consideration of our times and our society was the impulse springing from the simple conviction that this sort of unutterable barbarity should never happen again. In Jules Romain's *Verdun*—one of the best of all the war books, even though it came, or possibly because it came, long after the main mass had been read and buried away in the back of the mind—there is wrung from one of the characters the exclamation that nothing—*nothing*—could be worth all the suffering which he feels and sees around him. But it was not only the suffering, recorded on so many sensitive and courageous pages as well as upon those of the hysterical, of the radical propagandists, or of the merely prurient horror-merchants. Scattered through this great literature—the record of the first major war to be fought by armies almost universally literate and therefore able to record it—were books of another and in a way more dreadful kind. There was, for example, Colonel Repington's chatty, guileless account of the "inside" war—the war of gossip and intrigue, of cosy little tea parties and dinners among the great at which the lives of thousands were juggled on a clever remark, the war of petty ambitions, callousnesses, stupidities, all going on at the centers of power and command while men were dying not far away. There were books like Corday's diary of *The Paris Front,* with its bitterer, more adult cynicism and disillusion, its more acid picture of doubt and uncertainty in the ranks, of selfishness and smallness at the top. The suffering was bad enough. It was what had apparently gone on behind the suffering that made it worse. What, really, had it all been about? What were the real ends which this immense crucifixion of an age had served?

If the war raised the question, in the peace we seemed to have our answer. There were greed and littleness, silly nationalism, paltry personal ambition and plain unwisdom at Paris; and the Treaty of Versailles certainly was not perfect. But for me, and I imagine for a great many of my generation, it was not the Treaty, not anything which happened at Paris, that produced the real disillusion. It was what happened afterward. The statesmen may have been greedy and unwise; it was as nothing compared to the greed and folly and blindness of the peoples who were to pass upon their work. Many have now come to realize that the Treaty of Versailles, for all its faults, was in fact a much greater and nobler document than it was represented as being in the post-war years. But we younger people believed in the Treaty in 1920; most of us, I think, believed in the Covenant and the League, and in the new vistas which Wilson's high rhetoric had opened before us. Our elders pointed out the Treaty's faults. We were not impressed by them. We wanted to accept the great risks; we wanted to help build the new, warless world in which democratic institutions would not only be safe but would demonstrate a creative power beyond anything they had shown before. And we saw this vision dissipated before our eyes by a complicated, somehow grotesque, process which we did not understand. We saw it tangled in a partisan political battle about which most of us cared very little. We saw it picked elaborately to pieces by the destructive fingers of legalistic nicety; we saw it involved in absurd disputes about "the" League or "a" league; in manifestoes and reservations; in every kind of passionate inanity, sincere or otherwise. In the end, we did not quite know what had happened. We blamed it on the obstinacy of Wilson or the petty jealousy of Lodge; we wondered whether perhaps we had not been wrong ourselves, or ascribed the whole thing to the mere accidents of politics, to a malevolent chance. But the vision was dead, all right; there was no doubt about that, and not much doubt that, whatever personal contributions the politicians and editors had made to its destruction, it was the people themselves who had let it die. The steam had gone out of them. The ardor had evaporated. They could fight, suffer and win a war; they could put their victory to no intelligible purpose. They fled into "normalcy." They wanted to be let alone; to mumble all the old, easy shibboleths of patriotism and politics and economic reaction.

So it had all been for nothing. The speeches and flag-waving had been meaningless, or had meant only a barren and outworn kind of jingo patriotism. We may not have gone to war *for* an ideal, but an ideal had at least illuminated our course and given it the appearance of reasonableness. This ideal had vanished; in its place we had Warren G. Harding. It was not simply that the ideal had been betrayed by politicians or sold by evil men; it had been abandoned by the whole society of which we were a part. We were told by our elders, including those of unquestioned integrity and eminence, that to imagine that it was possible to eliminate war from international society or create a new world order was to betray a childish naïveté, not to mention a gross ignorance of the Constitution. We supposed that we had been fighting, or preparing to fight, for peace and democracy; it was an absurd notion—what we had really been fighting for was to take vengeance on the Germans for having sunk a few American ships and killed a small number of American citizens, most of whom had been fully warned of their danger. That was a real cause for war. The rest was a windy and impracticable "idealism," which could only affect inexperienced minds. We believed this, most of us—how could we have done otherwise? We might not have believed a Lodge, or even a Borah. But the election returns were unanswerable. The election returns were us; they were the voice of the society in which we were framed, by which alone we had our public existence. So it had all been, somehow, a mistake.

With this lesson, or what we could only read as this lesson, we were dumped into the post-war world; and, as I have said, it is not surprising if a good many of us felt that in the elimination of this pointless horror from society there lay the first, the central, problem of our times. The post-war world was in fact a much more confusing place than we knew. Its manners, its politics, its economy alike were in a much greater state of flux than we realized; the ancient issues between the individual and the state, between man and his society, were running so very deep that most of us were but dimly aware that there were any such issues at all. It was easy to fall victim to over-simple solutions. No doubt too many men and women of my generation relapsed into the simplest solution of all; they adopted a purely personal attitude toward their times, took what the day brought, voted the Democratic ticket or the Republican, tried to make a living and let it go at that. Of those troubled by a more restless impulse to understand their age, some simply forgot about the war and—taking up again at the point where everything had been dropped in 1914—concentrated their attention on all the old social issues, political reform, industrial relations, problems of economic and financial organization. But to others among us it seemed as if all that could wait. We forgot about society and concentrated our attention on war.

This loathsome atrocity, appalling in itself, destructive of all social values, with so much seeming baseness in its inspiration and futility in its results—this thing, surely, would have to be done away with. This, surely, was the one greatest scourge to which our civilization was still subject, more terrible than poverty, more crushing than injustice, productive of more waste and misery and degradation than all the special ills which formed the stuff of peace-time socio-economic controversy. So a good many of us felt; and we attacked our enemy in our several ways. Some, like Hemingway or Dos Passos or Stallings, reported the horror as they had seen it with a passionate and convincing indignation. Some—Sherwood comes to mind—used the weapons of satire. Some journeyed to Geneva in Shotwell's trail; they gave themselves to the effort of reviving the war-time inspiration, of breathing life into the League of Nations, of elaborating new legal formulae—"outlawries of war," "collective securities," perfected "peace systems"—in which to bind the monster. Others, like Buell, founded or labored in study associations, tried to stimulate thought or spread information, wrote monographs, compiled statistics. It was a war on a wide front. The historical process had demonstrated to us that the original war against war for which we had enlisted had not really been that at all; we had simply allowed ourselves to be bamboozled by the propagandas. But, as Keynes once said of Wilson, we refused to be de-bamboozled. This was our own war against war. Events have proved that it was a misdirected one. But none, I think, who took however small a part in it need be ashamed of having done so.

I had a part in it; I do not pretend that it was a particularly important one, but this is admittedly autobiography. I am using myself simply as an illustration to show that the men and women of the "war generation" have in their own way been through most of the dilemmas that appear to trouble their immediate successors; whatever we may say now is at any rate not said in ignorance of those issues or blindness toward them. Like these others in the middle post-war years I was fascinated by the subject of war; I loathed the business; I thought an attack upon it as good a point as any other at which to attack the general problem of our times. Most of the excuses advanced to justify militaristic preparation and war-like policies seemed to me obviously shallow—the transparent rationalizations of people either blinded by their vested interest in military institutions or incapable of taking more than a childishly narrow, romantic view of human history. I remember the disgust with which I followed, for example, the antics of the "Coolidge" naval conference in 1927, at which unthinking jingo nationalism, professional navalist pedantry and a total failure to bring any scientific analysis to the question of what the proposed ships were really for or really capable of doing, succeeded—not, it may be said, without the assistance of the munitions interests—in wrecking any chance of completing the structure of naval limitation which had been begun at Washington in 1921. I was as critical as most of military measures, military appropriations, the whole inspiration and purpose of the military institution. And it occurred to me to write my own kind of book about war.

It was in 1931 that I published a book called *The Martial Spirit*. It was an account of the Spanish-American War, written partly because this seemed to me in itself a curious and arresting episode in the development of contemporary America, but partly, also, because it seemed a suggestive example of the war process in action. I was inclined to think of war as a disease or aberration of normal society; and though the whole emphasis of this book was satiric rather than solemn, I felt that it might be of use as a kind of practical case-history. Precisely because the scale of the Spanish-American War was small, the physical horrors relatively few, but the historical consequences considerable, it should offer a better subject in which to study the essential pathology than the vaster, more complex and more terrible examples. The book did not go unread. But if it was a case history, it never suggested to me—nor to anyone else so far as I am aware—any hint of the cure.

Perhaps war was not, as I and many others had tended to regard it, a disease of society. Perhaps it was not even a crime, as the authors of the Treaty of Versailles had assumed and as the earnest workers in the Geneva vineyards still seemed to assume. Perhaps it was a stupidity—a failure in logic and sense on the part of peoples and their responsible statesmen, a vast accident compounded out of short-sightedness, ignorance, the inability to relate means to end or cause to effect. So, at any rate, the outbreak of war in 1914 seemed to have been, as it was now appearing to us through the researches of Fay and the other scholars of the "origins." I was struck by the fact that I did not know either how or why the United States had got into the war in 1917; I was even more struck by the fact that no one else seemed to know either. Plenty of people had their explanations, of course, but the explanations were all different; there were any number of reasons, but when they were all added up they did not come to anything very reasonable. I decided that I would try to find out, to my own satisfaction at any rate; and I went to work upon another book, the primary purpose of which was simply to give as full, as intelligible and self-consistent an account as I could of the "origins" of the American intervention.

Again it seemed to me that the attempt might yield a book which would not only be of interest in itself but would be useful. I felt that one great trouble with everyone dabbling in this subject—from the peace-society people at one end with their simple denunciations of war around through the Geneva legalists with their protocols and "peace systems" to the soldiers, whose one prescription was more armaments to preserve the peace—was that they all had an inadequate grasp of the actual process which they were trying to control. They were, so to speak, proposing to regulate a watch with no more imaginative an understanding of its anatomy than could be derived from a cursory glance at the movement. Each was so sure that they knew how the watch ought to work, and therefore how to regulate it, that none was taking time to find out whether the watch really did work that way. In the case of the American intervention in 1917, I wanted to find out how the watch had actually ticked, what had made it go, what kind of mechanisms were involved. Except for a powerful bias against avoidable wars, I really had no bias in this endeavor; I was not committed to any single theory of the war's causation, but I did hope that from a survey of the war mechanisms as a whole there might emerge some practical hints as to how to control these mechanisms—if not for the complete prevention of war, then at least so as to insure that they would yield less socially futile results than seemed to have been achieved in this case.

It was not our entry in the war which I minded so much; it was what I regarded as our complete betrayal afterward of everything which might have justified the sacrifice and made the victory worth while. But the subsequent betrayal might have resulted from an initial confusion as to the purposes for which we had taken up the sword. And the more I looked into it the more was I impressed by how much confusion there had been. Applying the light of after-knowledge to the actual causes of the American entry, I saw everywhere what seemed to me to be short-sightedness, ignorance, passionate emotionalism, personal (if often unconscious) greeds or political ambitions, a reckless, almost frivolous, failure to analyze the actual situation at any given time so as to utilize the great power of the United States in such a way as to achieve concrete results in some degree equivalent to the inevitable costs of any given course of action. When it was completed, my book, *Road to War,* was a pretty severe indictment of the whole process; *that* war, I felt, should have been prevented, and I thought I detected in the analysis not a few points at which better controls might have been applied, not a few ways in which the war mechanism might have been so regulated as either to have avoided the intervention altogether or at least insured that any intervention we might have made would have achieved far more at far less cost.

The book got read. It did seem to influence some people—it may have helped to influence some policies. I never imagined, and would not for a moment claim, that I supplied the inspiration for the neutrality acts of 1935 and later. But *Road to War* appeared at a time when others had begun to re-examine the 1914–1917 period for suggestions as to how in fact to prevent a repetition of that episode. They had detected much the same points as I thought I found for the application of controls that might have "kept the country out of war" then and that might serve to do so in face of the new storms that by this time were gathering in Europe. A good many abler and more influential minds that my own were concerned with the problem; if I speak of my own share in it, it is again only because this is illustrative autobiography. But whatever my share may have been, the results were not entirely satisfactory to myself. The more it came to the point of trying to translate the suggested controls—embargoes, restrictions on loans, discouragements to propaganda and so on—into concrete legislative policy which would meet a future situation that was beyond exact prediction, the more difficult did the undertaking appear. I wrote some articles and made a number of speeches about neutrality and how to maintain it, but it never seemed to me that I succeeded in saying much. In the end a number of the suggestions implicit in my book (as in other studies of the subject) were written into law. But the several neutrality acts were obviously fumbling and confused creations; they began to be applied, in the Ethiopian, the Far Eastern and the Spanish crises, in some very peculiar and unexpected ways, and it seemed as if something, somewhere, must have been left out of the demonstration.

It was. In the end about all that this particular line of attack had yielded were some suggestions as to technical devices that would assist in keeping the country out of war—provided it wanted to stay out of the war. They were, in other words, devices which would not really be of much practical use except in conditions under which they would hardly be necessary. They might do something toward preventing an abandonment of neutrality for trivial, frivolous, purely momentary, reasons; they nowhere reached to the basic problem of war itself. They said nothing about the fundamental reasons for which nations do or do not fight. Granting that I had proved in my book (I did to my own satisfaction, if not to that of others) that the United States had blundered in a blind and confused way into the last war, and in so doing had doomed its intervention to a large measure of futility, I still had not proved that it might not go clear-sightedly into another war, and thereby achieve results, in terms of national or human welfare, that would be commensurate with the cost. For that matter, I had not even proved that it would not have been an even greater disaster had we stayed out of the last war than it was to go into it. If I had suggested something as to possible means for controlling the war process, I had said nothing whatever about the ends to which the controls should be applied. I had said nothing about the actual role of war in human society; neither had most others. The very people who were most vociferous in their determination that the United States should never under any circumstances enter another European war were the first to assume it as axiomatic that the country would have to fight if invaded. But why the one and not the other? The answer was by no means so obvious as it appeared to be at first sight.

And all the while such questions were growing only more and not less urgent. While we talked and wrote books and adopted resolutions and devised "peace systems," the distant thunders were muttering steadily louder, steadily more insistent. In this brief sketch of our own private "war to end war" I have scarcely mentioned what was going on in the world at the same time—the rise of military Fascism, the slow disintegration of the League of Nations, the world depression, the invasion of Manchuria, the enthronement of Nazism in supreme power over Germany. It might seem as though I were describing a campaign conducted in a vacuum. It might seem so; and unfortunately that, I believe, is exactly what it was. As I said before, we forgot about society to concentrate our attention upon war. It was war in the abstract we thought about—war in general, an entity to be set aside and examined and combated in itself. This was true, whether we thought of it as a disease, a crime, a stupidity or a mechanical process. In each case we were isolating war from the society in which it appears; and I think that the hard-bitten economic determinists among us—the Marxists who regarded it as an inevitable product of the capitalistic system or the radical materialists who ascribed it most rigorously to such alleged social forces as imperialist rivalry, pressures of population and so on—were doing so just as much as the rest of us. However much they may have fallen back on social forces for their explanation, it was still war in the abstract—war as a thing in itself—of which they were thinking. But war is not abstract, nor a thing in itself. It does not simply grow out of society; in a sense, it *is* society. It is certainly the most striking, and the most completely socialized, of all social activities. We were making a double error. We were at the same time both isolating our subject too rigorously from its social context, and generalizing it too loosely, assuming on the one hand that war could be treated as a thing in itself and on the other hand that all wars were the same kind of thing. One phrase has re-echoed now for years through American life: "We must keep the United States out of war." But two obvious questions have rarely been asked: "Who are 'we'?" and "What war?" Had they been asked more often, we might have made more progress.

We did not ask them; but history did. We had been opposing war in the abstract; Herr Hitler, improving enormously upon the initiatives already taken by Mussolini, by the Russians and the rest, abruptly presented it to us in a very concrete form. We had assumed that all reasonable men were one in wishing to eliminate wars from the world. Here were men—I will not say whether they were reasonable or not, but they were men who had raised themselves to absolute power over great nations—who were deliberately cultivating war as the central framework of society. They had made it the operating principle of the state, the primary social institution binding all others together. War was as fundamental to the totalitarian state as the concept of majority rule or legal process was to the democratic type of social organization. Their economy was based on armament orders; their politics on military discipline; their social aims on imperial conquest; their foreign policy on all the cruel myths—racial superiority, survival of the fittest, population pressure, the necessity to expand and so on—which had been used to rationalize warfare in the past and which we had labored so long to expose.

We had hated the physical suffering and horror of war; it meant nothing to these men. We had hated the febrile emotionalism, the propaganda lies and exaggerations essential to its conduct by the complex modern state. They made the lie a main instrument of government and elevated propaganda to a religious dogma. We had hated the intellectual suppressions of war, its barbarous blindness and narrowness. They clapped an iron censorship on their people. We had hated war's release of the most primitive passions, the sadism and blood lust to which it gave expression. They had used sadism as a motivating force of their society, and while foreign enemies were unavailable as victims they had quite deliberately appointed their Jewish communities to the role. We had hated, or thought we had hated, war's complete overriding of the individual, its imposition of an absolute unity. They perceived in this aspect of war one of its deepest and most powerful appeals to the lonely human spirit; and while they jammed their concentration camps with the recalcitrant they put all the rest of their people, down to their girls and babies, into uniform. And out of these elements they compounded a social organization of amazing strength, stability and destructive energy.

Here was war in a concrete form which we had not anticipated. Before this development all our arguments fell to the ground. War is horrible? "Of course," they replied in effect, "what of it?" and they burned all the books, barred all the motion picture films and jammed all the radio broadcasts which might have conveyed this degenerate notion to their own people. Your whole picture of the world is a cruel and grotesque lie? "Naturally," they responded, "so is yours; but ours is a bigger lie and so more readily believed. We will make it bigger still. We will make it such a thundering lie that we shall believe it ourselves and then nothing can touch us." And the trouble was that they were, in a measure, right. Their system worked. It worked to ends that seemed brutal, retrogressive, destructive to us, but it worked; and nothing that we could say—nothing that we had said in the twenty-odd years we had been pondering these problems—had the slightest relevance to the issue.

Here there was not only war in a new form; here was rapidly developing a specific war. We saw it coming nearer and nearer, in China and Ethiopia and Spain and Austria; and nothing in the armory which we had elaborated against war in general had any effect upon the steady advance of this particular conflict. The final demonstration was slow to arrive. The democratic statesmen used all the weapons against war which we had suggested. They were patient; they were reasonable; they refused to take bellicose action; they were slow to build up their own armaments; they tried to see the other side's point of view; they offered concessions. And still the crisis developed. At last there was Munich. Mr. Chamberlain, in effect, took our advice. He was not going to waste human life for small, uncertain and ignoble ends. What, in any rational system of human accounting, was the fate of Czechoslovakia worth to the young Englishmen who would have to die to save her? What had war ever achieved except disaster and destruction for all? Who could win a modern war, about which the only certain thing was that everyone would be a loser? Mr. Chamberlain applied these principles, which so many of us had so often elaborated, to the case in hand. Mr. Chamberlain did not fight; he did not waste life—and within some eighteen months Europe was filled with the dead bodies of Poles and Finns and Norwegians and Frenchmen and Englishmen and Germans by the hundreds of thousands; the giant bombs were smashing English pubs and churches and homes, the wreck and waste of war was spread over a continent.

Here was the demonstration; and it was convincing. We were no longer facing war in general; here was war, specific and concrete, and it was war offering no quarter, admitting of no compromise. The only way to combat it was to fight it in the literal sense, with its own weapons—bombs, machine-guns, tanks, and a passionate determination however engendered, whether by patriotism, by propaganda, by hope of a better world, by fear of a worse one, or by the simple resolve to do one's share in a common job the doing of which cannot be avoided. Here was the demonstration, and here was the dilemma. One had either to fight war by making oneself warlike—by embracing all the cruelties, the suppressions, the agonies which we had detested—or one had to surrender to it and see it enthroned in the world as the central institution of Western civilization, and the world itself organized, directed and controlled by the barbarous men who had built the New Europe around it.

Here was the dilemma; and at the first moment it seemed an appalling one. To many it still seems so. It has terrified some, paralyzed others and driven many more into a weak evasion of the issue which is perhaps worse than paralysis. Those who say that we shall never fight in Europe but will of course defend our national territory against invasion are among them. They merely hope that there will never be an invasion; and hiding their eyes in this hope, which is none too solid at best, they refuse to see that once the possibility of fighting at all is admitted, the question of the point at which to fight becomes almost a technical one—a practical question of achieving maximum gain at minimum cost. Those are also among them who talk of piling our own armaments to the skies while making peace with whoever wins in Europe. They are evading the whole issue as Mr. Chamberlain did when he came back from Munich with "peace in our time" and a redoubled rearmament program. Why armaments if we are to make peace, and why peace if we need armaments? What are the armaments supposed to be for? What are they to defend—a mere geographical entity, or a way of life, a general system of political and social ideas, which any peace with a victorious Hitler would certainly make impossible?

There have been many in these past few months who, in all sorts of ways, have been desperately trying to evade their whole problem or hide it from themselves. They do not want to fight and they do not want to surrender; they are very anxious to prepare, but they do not know what the preparedness is to defend, and they shudder when practically effective steps are proposed —such as the prompt occupation of bases, an embargo against Japan, an alliance with Canada, the despatch of ships or American air squadrons to Britain—which hold out some hope of making the preparedness really effective at minimum long-run cost. But some of us, who after all have lived with this thing a good while now, have begun to ask ourselves some of these rather fundamental questions. Why, for example, should one be denounced as a blood-thirsty warmonger for suggesting that a few thousand Americans should be enlisted now to tip the scales of history where they are hanging balanced on the coasts of England; and yet everybody assume it to be axiomatic that, should the scales go down, we would draft not only New Yorkers but Georgians and Californians to die in far greater numbers for the defense of New York? Why should there be such a determined insistence on the volunteer system of raising an army when no one has ever suggested a volunteer system for raising taxes? Why should we think it admirable to persuade, entice or browbeat our more impressionable young men into dying for us, when if anyone is to be asked to die it can surely only be because this is an imperative duty which each owes equally to the whole?

And in asking such questions as these—I throw them out at random—not only does the dilemma cease to be a dilemma at all, but at last, I think, we begin to approach the heart of this problem with which we have wrestled for twenty-odd years. War loses none of its hideousness or horror. But it is seen clearly to be something which reaches to the very fundamentals of our state and our society. You cannot ask poor men to suffer and die for nothing more than the rich man's profits; you cannot enlist one man to suffer and leave his neighbor free to enjoy in comfort all the benefits of his sacrifice. You cannot adopt a cautious foreign policy in order to save the lives of a few thousand today if by doing so you are going to slaughter hundreds of thousands tomorrow; similarly, you cannot draft millions to exhaust their time and energy in preparation for defense if you are going to give away everything that you have taught them to believe in defending. War challenges virtually every other institution of society—the justice and equity of its economy, the adequacy of its political systems, the energy of its productive plant, the bases, wisdom and purposes of its foreign policy. There is no aspect of our existence as individuals living in and by virtue of a social group which is not touched, modified, perhaps completely altered by the imperatives of war. And that is only to say, as I have said before, that war *is* society. It is society in action, for defense or aggression. Whether we like it or not it is, at the present stage of human history, virtually our one completely social activity; and so long as it exists in the world we cannot, as social beings, escape it.

We had thought of war as something distinct from the normal operations of society—a special case of disease or crime or stupidity. But while I believe it to partake of all those attributes, it is not special or distinct. It is, as yet, the deepest expression of our social life, and as social beings we have to face it. The young man, for example, who resents being drafted for a year's military service because it will interfere with his career can with justice, I think, be asked why he assumes that he will have a career, if he is uninterested in the common defense of the social framework which alone makes any modern career a possibility. War is society; and there are still times when any social organization—as the French have just demonstrated with terrible completeness—must be willing to fight unless it is to die. I do not think this will always be so. The war to end war must and will go on and ultimately I believe it will be victorious. But war cannot be conquered by those who are afraid of it; and no great social ends can ever be achieved by those who are unable to act as members of their own society, utilizing when it is unavoidable the forms of expression, however gross or cruel, through which a social group does in fact operate as a society and not merely as a random collection of individuals.

This may seem illogical; I do not care if it does. For if our first error was to approach war as a thing in itself, our second was to approach it as a purely rational issue. We demanded of this horror that it must have a reason to justify it, quite forgetting that almost no aspect of human life ever is reasonable. If governments are to lead their peoples into war, we said, they must do so in the highest wisdom, in complete purity of motive and for ends not only clearly conceived but worth the sacrifice; and when greed or cowardice or littleness appeared here and there behind the lines we flamed with disgust and disillusion. The disgust was appropriate; the disillusion was naïve. Greed and littleness and unwisdom are the commonplaces of all existence; no triumph of peace has ever been achieved without their presence, and while the effort to reduce them should be unrelenting, their existence should neither cause surprise nor be an excuse for defeatism.

The suffering, we said, must have a reason, and were exasperated when we could find none to assign to it. We forgot the amount of quite irrational suffering in all existence. There are disasters, losses, bitter bereavements in peacetime life—completely aimless, unjust and no less difficult to bear than those imposed by war. The suffering of war is a great reason for trying to do away with war; but we will never do away with war by expecting it to be rational, and to say that it is not is no excuse for failing to fight it with its own weapons, the only weapons, as we have been taught, which give any promise of success.

We are not rationalists discussing a problem in logic. We are men and women living social lives, utilizing for ends that seem good to us the instruments which society has developed. There is perfection nowhere, either in means or results, and there is suffering everywhere. But we know that no social life of any sort is possible unless it is informed by convictions—convictions which can never in the end be justified rationally but convictions at least so strong that we are prepared, when there is no alternative, to fight and take the risk of dying for them. And we must be prepared to do this, not as a result of a bargain—I will risk my neck in an airplane if you guarantee that my children will live in peace, security, enlightenment and on a good income—but simply because we are partners in a common, social effort, and the thing has to be done if we are to do anything. I suggested before that perhaps the best of all reasons for enlisting is that everybody else is doing it; the reason that when there is a common job to be done we wish to have our part in its doing.

The American way of life has many faults and blemishes; it also has many things about it that one may hold up as worth fighting for and risking death for—its freedoms, its decencies, its strivings toward a better existence for greater numbers of its people, its effort to utilize as the springs of its social and political system the highest rather than the basest, the most advanced rather than the most primitive, instinctual drives in humanity. But great as these things are, and imminent though the present threat to them may be, I still do not think we can offer them as the sole, or even the primary, reason for again taking up the sword or again being prepared to do so. If our attitude is purely defensive, if we are merely sitting hoarding our liberties against threatened attack, those liberties are only too likely to atrophy anyway. If we try to make a bargain out of it, if we say to our countrymen, "you must be ready to fight in order to preserve your freedom, in order to enjoy this or that benefit of a democratic as opposed to a totalitarian system, in order to safeguard the nation against invasion," we may always find that the reasons do not particularly appeal. Men's values inevitably differ, and in the last analysis are always irrational, beyond assessment by any form of cost accounting in which such-and-such an amount of pain or death can be equated to such-and-such a quantity of human or social advance. It is not, really, that kind of calculation at all. But suppose we say: "You must be ready to fight; if you are that; if the society of which you are a part has that much cohesion, conviction and energy as a social whole, then perhaps you will have a chance to make good your freedoms, to avoid the crimes of totalitarian retrogression, really to preserve your nation and whatever of its values seem best to you from foreign invasion—and to do all these things probably with far less cost in life and suffering than if you confess your social organization to be a weak and spineless thing, a mere collection of individual selfishnesses." Suppose we say that. I think we are much closer to the facts both of war and of social organization as a whole; I think we are much nearer to putting our hands upon the primary levers that operate the world we live in. We are then moving with, and not in puny revolt against, the main stream of human existence. We are not then merely kicking against the machinery which drives it; we are not, with the totalitarians, developing all the crudest, most primitive and most wasteful elements of that machinery in order easily to establish a barren power; but we are utilizing the basic mechanisms to produce, in time, better machinery, better results, a better ultimate life.

We are doing our part. I have a feeling that it is worth doing for itself, and in that feeling the dilemma seems to me to disappear. If war can only be fought by making war upon it, then I am prepared to make war upon it. And I doubt whether any other great social end can be achieved unless one is ready at least to risk one's life, as a unit in the social mechanism, for its attainment. I have put all this in generalized, one might say philosophical terms. It seems to me no less true if it is translated into the most rigidly practical ones. Given the existing world situation as of today, I do not know, I am sure, whether the United States can avoid war, death, destruction; whether it can maintain the essentials of liberal-democratic institutions, a reasonably free, full and prosperous life for its people or not. But it seems to me, as a purely practical calculation in politico-diplomatic probabilities, that the United States will have a far better chance of doing all these things, of utilizing its power to achieve maximum gains at minimum costs, if it can now rely upon a people who feel themselves one, who are ready to do any jobs that require doing, who are prepared in the last analysis to fight if need be and die if they must, who do not shudder in humanitarian horror over a small sacrifice of life if it offers any real and practical chance of averting much greater sacrifices, who have first of all the energy to act as a people, and after that the resolve to utilize the action toward great and not little ends.